Growing Up and Parenting:
Two score and Four Years Ago

Collected by David Paraiso
Copyrighted (2013)

Book Cover Description:

This book is a collection of growing up and parenting narratives from medical doctors, professors, managers, accountants, nurse, researcher, financial analyst, engineer, consultant and mentor – who graduated from the UEC High School Two Score and Four Years ago. The 10 narratives and supporting materials share the "lessons learned" and "best practices" as well as the shortcomings and tragedies from childhood to adolescence, to adulthood, into the 40s, 50s, 60s, and the golden years – which are timeless and repeated by each generation across communities, cultures and borders. The stories are intended as reference materials and transformative roadmap for adolescents, would-be parents, parents, guardians, mentors, teachers, social workers, and other parties who have an interest in the adversities, challenges and in managing growing up and parenting.

This book is a response to one conundrum of our times where we have courses and training for just about everything from "French cooking" to "jungle survival", but very few if any, are in the area of growing up and parenting.

Being sensitive to the value of time and with a sense of urgency, the organizers and narrators wanted their collective experiences and messages be articulated in a focused, brief, non-technical, comprehensive and cohesive manner that will not exceed 100 pages at a high level. Fully digesting and appreciating the contents of the book, however, will take many more hours and days as one listens to the music, reads the verses, watches the movies and surfs the links listed in the book. Implementing and executing a plan of action will take a life-time - cradle to grave, across generations.

For optimal effect, it is recommended that you complete reading the Introduction portion of this book prior to reading each narrative. This book takes a multi-media approach which facilitates experiencing and endearing the "lessons learned" and "best practices" from the narratives by reading sections of the book, clicking on the links for background information, listening to the music at youtube.com, watching the movies, and conducting discussions on what resonated the most. It will take several sessions to complete this process together; this is a journey.

Reasonable effort was exerted in acknowledging the materials referenced in this book – from various composers, artists, poets, speakers, thinkers, writers, historians, mentors, role models and many others. Their contribution is priceless and treasured for articulating the universality of the human experience across communities, cultures, generations and millennia. Our sincerest and most profound thanks and appreciation to all of them.

TABLE OF CONTENTS

Introduction

The contents of this book are intended as reference materials and roadmap for adolescents, would-be parents, parents, guardians, mentors, teachers, social workers, and other parties who have an interest in the adversities, challenges and in managing growing up and parenting.

This book is a collection of 10 narratives - passing to the next generations - the growing up experience, "lessons learned" and "best practices" as well as the shortcomings and tragedies from childhood to adolescence, adulthood, into the 40s, 50s, 60s, and the golden years.

Reasonable effort was exerted in acknowledging the materials referenced in this book – the composers, artists, poets, speakers, thinkers, writers, historians, mentors, role models and many others. Their contribution is priceless and treasured for articulating the universality of the human experience across cultures, generations and millennia. Our sincerest and profound thanks and appreciation to all of them.

For optimal effect, it is recommended that you complete reading the Introduction portion of this book prior to reading each narrative. This book takes a multi-media approach which facilitates experiencing and endearing the "lessons learned" and "best practices" from the narratives by reading sections of the book aloud in front of an audience, clicking on the links for background information, listening to the music at youtube.com, watching the movies, and conducting a discussion on what resonated the most. It will take several sessions to complete this process together; this is journey.

BACKGROUND

Two score and 4 years ago are 44 years. In 1969, or 44 years ago, the University of the East Caloocan High School batch of 1969 (UECHS-69) graduated. The narrators were between 14 and 16 olds at that time. Now, in 2013, they are in their early 60s. Since graduation in 1969 - through their children and their children, through the children of their siblings, cousins, peers, friends, neighbors and associates – they experienced, and witnessed generations after generations transition from being toddlers, to childhood, adolescence, adulthood, and eventually, the golden years. This has been a 44 year voyage of discovery and serendipity. The organizers and narrators wanted to complete this pilot while they still could, and while they are in touch with their batchmates.

The UECHS is a private high school catering to middle-middle class, working class, and struggling families. There are other schools catering to the rich and upper middle class families. In reviewing the narratives, it is apparent that this humble beginning did not hinder several of the UECHS graduates from excelling and reaching the top of their respective fields of specialization.

WHAT TRIGGERED THE WRITING OF THE BOOK?

This book is one of the deliverables of the UECHS-69 pilot. The planning for the pilot commenced several weeks prior to the scheduled June 22, 2013 UECHS-69 reunion in Las Vegas, Nevada. Besides the activities, pleasantries and excitement normally associated with such reunions, 44 years after the 1969 batch graduated from high school, there are those who wanted something more focused, endearing, encompassing, lasting and easily digestible that could be passed from this increasingly rare gathering to the next generations. Pass on a legacy is one way to describe this aspiration.

The organizers firmly believe that there are aspects of individual and shared experience, which are re-learned and repeated in each generation across cultural, ethnic, religious, gender-orientation, and national boundaries. Most of the narrators encountered adversities and challenges particularly during adolescent years. There are sensitive topics covered in this book which were not talked about, or there were no guidance available, or these were considered taboo subjects when they were growing up. Because of these, several narrators paid dearly for these gaps. This said, the next generations and interested parties could benefit from the contents of this book.

Being sensitive to the value of time and of utmost urgency, the organizers and narrators wanted their collective experiences and messages be articulated in a focused, brief, non-technical, comprehensive and cohesive manner that are will not exceed 100 pages at a high level. Fully digesting and appreciating the contents the book, however, could take many more hours and days as one listens to the music, reads the verses, watches the movies and surfs the links listed in the book. Implementing and executing a plan of action will take a life-time - cradle to grave, across generations.

Each narrative is intended to be a 20-40 minute verbal story of each narrator covering the most significant and memorable events, and focusing on what could be passed along.

INTRODUCING THE NARRATORS

- o The Farmer's Son (Bank Business Manager)
- o The Office Wife (Administrative Assistant to the Director, School of Medicine, University of California, San Francisco)
- o The Zumba Girl (Nurse at Kaiser Permanente)
- o The Good Daughter from North Carolina (Accountant)
- o The Lioness Maiden (Division Manager of a Government Agency)
- o The Psychiatrist from California

- The Doctor from Tampa, Florida (Faculty at University of South Florida College of Medicine)
- The Doctor from Caloocan
- The Dreamer (Accountant and USAF Reserve from California)
- The Mentor from California

PILOT APPROACH AND ASSUMPTIONS

- Through face-to-face interaction, phone calls, direct email, mailing lists and facebook, volunteers from the UECHS-69 batch were invited to document and share their narratives. Managing a pilot of this nature - 44 years after the batch graduates last saw each other, across 15 time zones from several countries; working with volunteers who did not have a track record of working together 44 years ago; with varied motivations, orientation and proficiencies; with conflicting mindsets, temperaments and priorities; and, with personal privacy or confidentiality concerns – was a major undertaking and a formidable challenge.

  - From the start of the pilot, a set of objectives, operating guidelines and strong governance were defined and vigorously enforced and refined. Narratives which met deadlines and minimal performance standards are included in this book.

  - The operating guidelines allowed and encouraged each narrator to use a style of writing she/he feels most comfortable with for as long at the intended contents are there.

- This pilot is expected to be a voyage and journey of discovery and serendipity, with both intended and unintended consequences. During the pilot, there were numerous "Oh My God!" (OMG), "Eureka" and "You've got to be Kidding" moments among the pilot narrators and organizers.
- This pilot is subject to the principles of diminishing return. In a closed community like this high school batch, there are things that should remain a secret, or remain compartmentalized, otherwise this could doom the pilot.
- There are risks in undertaking this pilot - like reigniting old wounds, and triggering new ones; the trauma of recalling unpleasant events, uncovering skeletons in the closet, etc. But, if managed properly, with highly focused objectives, deliverables, and with a carefully selected set of volunteers, the benefits will far outweigh the risks.
- The narrators tried their best to capture the successes, failures, struggles, adversities, challenges, tragedies – and how each of them coped and managed the process. Doing anything less than this is incomplete, presumptuous, and will undermine the objectives and the integrity of the pilot.

  - The narratives captured the dispositions, character flaws, deficiencies and vulnerabilities, particularly during their adolescent years. Where possible and appropriate, taboo subjects were also covered. Because these were not priorities, or there was lack of knowledge on these subjects when the narrators were growing up, they grew up at their own peril!

- None of the organizers or narrators is a professional writer, nor do any of them claim to be such. However, what they lack in writing proficiencies, they make up in terms of substance and depth – they have an abundance of personal stories, forged and tested by time, sweat, tears and blood - which were generously shared in their own words and style with the intended audiences.
- Based on what was known of other graduating batches, there are rare factors and opportunities – in terms of trust, proficiencies, personalities, dynamics and readiness – with the batch of UECHS-69, which favor completing this pilot successfully. At least this was true of the reunion participants who met in June 2013, and the pilot volunteers.
- Several of the organizers and narrators are expected to continue writing and collaborating beyond the pilot because there is something appealing, therapeutic, uplifting, empowering and fulfilling in the process - compared to doing nothing or less.
- Organizers and narrators alike will be not being the same individuals coming out of this pilot, compared to when they first started.
- The pilot is expected to generate a different set of dynamics, and will spawn other initiatives down the line.
- To better appreciate the substance and depth of the insight and sentiment of the narrators, the readers and audiences are encouraged to listen to the musical pieces, understand the verses and lyrics, visit the internet links, and watch the movies provided in the book. Putting it another way, the musical pieces, the verses, lyrics, the movie characters and plots are integral parts of the narratives. This said, the electronic version of the book lends itself in facilitating connection to the URLs pointed to by the musical pieces, movies and various links.

OBSERVATIONS

The following summarize the narratives and interviews of the narrators. Several of these were not explicitly documented in the narratives but were shared with the author for the benefit of the intended audiences.

- During the transition to adolescent years, in one form or another, most narrators experienced being ignored, spurned, rejected or abandoned by their "crushes" or "love" or "those" whose attention and affection they desperately sought and craved for. This is particularly pronounced during adolescent years, and if not managed properly, this could a scar a person for life.
- From http://tweenparenting.about.com – "Adolescent egocentrism is teens' and older tweens' belief that others are highly attentive to their behavior and appearance. That is, egocentric adolescents believe that all eyes are on them.

Adolescent egocentrism is a developmentally normal cognitive limitation. In other words, teens and older tweens can no more stop themselves from being egocentric than an infant can fix their inability to speak. Adolescent egocentrism usually appears around 11 or 12 years of age and tapers off around 15 or 16 years."

- Peer group acceptance and appreciation are universal desires and aspirations – male or female. Just like "crushes" or "love", if this is not managed properly, the self-esteem of a person could be compromised for life, and which will cascade through generations.

  As an example, the current Pope Francis (Jorge Mario Bergoglio from Argentina) has said that as a young seminarian, he "was dazzled by a girl he met at an uncle's wedding", so much so that he "could not pray for over a week" because he could not help thinking of her, and so he "had to rethink what he was doing". As a Jesuit novice he studied humanities in Santiago, Chile. At the conclusion of his novitiate in the Society of Jesus, Bergoglio officially became a Jesuit on 12 March 1960, when he made the religious profession of the initial, temporary vows of a member of the order. For specifics, please refer to: http://en.wikipedia.org/wiki/Pope_Francis.

- From Miguel de Unamuno - "Love is the child of illusion and the parent of disillusion". From Rita Rudner - "I love being married. It's so great to find one special person you want to annoy for the rest of your life". From Goethe - "Love is an ideal thing, marriage a real thing; a confusion of the real with the ideal never goes unpunished'. From W. Somerset Maugham - "Perfection is what American women expect to find in their husbands... but English women only hope to find in their butlers".

- Several of the narrators were "animated lovers". Though they had been imbued with, and had a checklist of what constitute an "ideal love", each of them experienced temporary madness when they met a match who got them to behave in ways not worthy of "rational or cultured beings". In several of these encounters, the best came out; while in some encounters, the worst came out. What is this mystic about love that makes rational beings behave irrationally, and irrational beings behave worse? In this context, love is like designer drugs.

- The male narrators experienced bullying and harassments. The female narrators did not report bullying but they did talk about not being accepted by groups whose affection they seek.

- Each generation repeats the same mistakes and missteps over and over again.

- If you sit all of batch mates next to each other in a plane or auditorium for 16 consecutive hours, most of the UECHS graduates will hardly recognize each other 44 years after graduation.

- Sustained and strong support system and network during the most critical times are often decisive in determining the long-term success of an individual.

- There are relationships worth defending and fighting for at all costs through the peaks and valleys, feast and famine, and the celebrations and tragedies of life. However, there are also relationships that simply take space and time, and do not really add value and are not worth keeping. These are relationships where one feels good about, and by the time one realizes that it was a drag, one is either too old to do anything about it, or too many opportunities had been lost that are not going to come again. The immediate challenges are: (1) distinguishing one from the other; and, (2) having the discipline to maintain and nurture the one that is worth keeping. It does not take much to damage a valued relationship – an off guard comment, a seemingly innocent and trivial misunderstanding which morphed into a federal case, a rumor, manipulation by an outside party, etc.

- 44 years ago at UECHS, the following were true:

  - There were no programs for at risk or special needs adolescents.
  - There were no mentoring or support groups.
  - There were no social media networks.
  - Important adolescent topics were considered as taboo subjects.

As a result, several of the narrators temporarily lost their way and it took some time for them to recover.

- Once upon a time, we were all toddlers. Being toddlers are captured by "Twinkle Twinkle Little Star":

http://www.youtube.com/watch?v=dCFs-0B5X2E

Twinkle, twinkle, little star,
How I wonder what you are.
Up above the world so high,
Like a diamond in the sky.

When the blazing sun is gone,
When he nothing shines upon,
Then you show your little light,
Twinkle, twinkle, all the night.

Then the traveler in the dark,
Thanks you for your tiny spark,
He could not see which way to go,
If you did not twinkle so.

(continued...)

- Then, love expectations during adolescent years are captured by "It Must Be Him" by Vicki Karr:

http://www.youtube.com/watch?v=kWvpJ5AY3mE

I tell myself what's done is done
I tell myself don't be a fool
Play the field have a lot of fun
It's easy when you play it cool

I tell myself don't be a chump
Who cares, let him stay away
That's when the phone rings and I jump
And as I grab the phone I pray

Let it please be him, oh dear God
It must be him or I shall die
Or I shall die
Oh hello, hello my dear God
It must be him but it's not him
And then I die
That's when I die

(continued...)

- Then, heart break is captured by "The End of the World" by Skeeter Davis:

  http://www.youtube.com/watch?v=NZ5WeXtOacU

  Why does the sun go on shining?
  Why does the sea rush to shore?
  Don't they know it's the end of the world?
  'Cause you don't love me any more

  Why do the birds go on singing?
  Why do the stars glow above?
  Don't they know it's the end of the world?
  It ended when I lost your love

  (continued...)

- Then, dreaming is captured by "Over the Rainbow" by Israel "IZ" Kamakawiwoʻole:

  http://www.youtube.com/watch?v=w_DKWlrA24k
  http://www.youtube.com/watch?v=R0xoMhCT-7A

  Ooh, ooh, ooh
  Ooh, ooh

  Somewhere over the rainbow

Way up high
And the dreams that you dream of
Once in a lullaby

Somewhere over the rainbow
Bluebirds fly
And the dreams that you dream of
Dreams really do come true

Someday, I wish upon a star
Wake up where the clouds are far behind me
Where trouble melts like lemon drops
High above the chimney top
That's where you'll find me

Somewhere over the rainbow
Bluebirds fly
And the dreams that you dare to
Oh why, oh why can't I?

Well, I see trees of green and red roses too
I'll watch them bloom for me and you
And I think to myself
What a wonderful world

(continued...)

- Our collective post-adolescent experience is captured by "Sunrise Sunset" from the Fiddler on the Roof:

  http://www.youtube.com/watch?v=nLLEBAQLZ3Q
  http://www.youtube.com/watch?v=nsQroDvqQAE

  Is this the little girl I carried? Is this the little boy at play?
  I don't remember growing older; When did they?
  When did she get to be a beauty? When did he grow to be so tall?
  Wasn't it yesterday; When they were small?
  Sunrise, sunset; Sunrise, sunset
  Swiftly flow the days; Seedlings turn overnight to sunflowers
  Blossoming even as we gaze

  (continued...)

- Holidays and family get together are captured by the "White Christmas" by Bing Crosby:

http://www.youtube.com/watch?v=aShUFAG_WgM

I'm dreaming of a white Christmas
Just like the ones I used to know
Where the tree tops glisten
And children listen
To hear sleigh bells in the snow

I'm dreaming of a white Christmas
With every Christmas card I write
May your days be merry and bright
And may all
Your Christmases be white

I'm dreaming of a white Christmas
Just like the ones I used to know
Where the tree tops glisten
And children listen
To hear sleigh bells in the snow

(continued...)

- Each time a loved one or batch mate fades away, the following music and lyrics resonate among us - "Going Home" by Dvorak:

http://www.youtube.com/watch?v=o2aLSat3h0w

Going home, going home
I'm jus' going home
Quiet like, some still day
I'm jus' going home

It's not far, yes close by
Through an open door
Work all done, care laid by
Going to fear no more

Mother's there 'specting me
Father's waiting, too
Lots of folk gathered there
All the friends I knew

All the friends I knew

I'm going home

(continued...)

- Comparing to what we were 44 years ago and 44 years later today: several of the graduates grew up, matured gracefully, and excelled in their respective specialties; there are those, who hardly grew up; and, sadly there are those who devolved.
- In mentoring, we cannot play God. It is best to limit our role to motivating, cheerleading, providing the tools, and creating the conditions for success; anything beyond these is a likely to be counterproductive. The rest will be up to the trainees or mentees. "You can lead a horse to water, but you can't make it drink."
- Several of the narrators were single parents who overcame unspeakable adversities and challenges along the way.
- Several of the narrators are high level performers and achievers in their fields, and could have achieved more career-wise but were not able to due to family obligations, insufficient resources and lack of support systems. This is particularly true among those who immigrated.
- The narratives in this book described how the pilot volunteers managed growing up with myriads of adversities and challenges along the way. There are those of us who have been wondering what happens to the millions of less fortunate orphans, children from dysfunctional families and those who are in foster homes or in the streets. This is a question to be answered for another time.
- Of the 10 narrators, 8 immigrated to the U.S., while 2 stayed in the land of our birth.
- Our collective message in this book is best captured by "Wonderful World" by Louis Armstrong and Israel "IZ" Kamakawiwoʻole :

http://www.youtube.com/watch?v=E2VCwBzGdPM
http://www.youtube.com/watch?v=R0xoMhCT-7A

I see trees of green........ red roses too
I see em bloom..... for me and for you
And I think to myself.... what a wonderful world.

I see skies of blue..... clouds of white
Bright blessed days....dark sacred nights
And I think to myself .....what a wonderful world.

The colors of a rainbow.....so pretty ..in the sky
Are also on the faces.....of people ..going by
I see friends shaking hands.....sayin.. how do you do
They're really sayin......I love you.

I hear babies cry...... I watch them grow
They'll learn much more.....than I'll never know

And I think to myself .....what a wonderful world

The colors of a rainbow.....so pretty ..in the sky
Are there on the faces.....of people ..going by
I see friends shaking hands.....sayin.. how do you do
They're really sayin...*spoken*(I ....love....you).

I hear babies cry...... I watch them grow
spoken(you know their gonna learn
A whole lot more than I'll never know)
And I think to myself .....what a wonderful world
Yes I think to myself ....what a wonderful world.

(continued...)

- Several universally shared experience that are most apparent from the narratives are: (1) regardless of age – the human character flaws, deficiencies and vulnerabilities; (2) the desire to survive and take care of their loved ones; (3) the desire to be accepted; (4) the desire to be loved; (5) strong aspiration to be successful.
- As part of the pilot, we collectively aspired to prove and reinforce that "the value of the whole is much more than the value of its individual components, and that there are things much greater than ourselves that we hardly appreciate and understand."

ACKNOWLEDGMENTS AND APPRECIATION

Reasonable effort was exerted in acknowledging the materials referenced in this book – the composers, artists, poets, speakers, thinkers, writers, historians, mentors, role models and many others. Their contribution is priceless and treasured for articulating the universality of the human experience across communities, cultures, generations and millennia. Our sincerest and profound thanks and appreciation to all of them.

We thank the volunteers of this pilot who took the time in reconstructing their past, and narrating their stories in their own style and words. It is worth noting that reconstructing the past included recalling traumatic experiences and events. Rightfully or wrongfully, our friendly and sustained harassment probably facilitated the process.

At the beginning of the pilot, there were questions if the book will be able to incorporate contents other than the cover and back pages, an introduction and 1 narrative. Over time, one baby step, led to another baby step, then to more steps, until sufficient momentum was achieved to complete the pilot.

For the narrators, our appreciation and thanks to them are best articulated by the song "Wind Beneath My Wings" by Bette Midler:

http://www.youtube.com/watch?v=5RMrltCDCwI
http://www.youtube.com/watch?v=VWqB-6ANG4c

Oh, oh, oh, oh, oh.
It must have been cold there in my shadow,
to never have sunlight on your face.
You were content to let me shine, that's your way.
You always walked a step behind.

So I was the one with all the glory,
while you were the one with all the strength.
A beautiful face without a name for so long.
A beautiful smile to hide the pain.

Did you ever know that you're my hero,
and everything I would like to be?
I can fly higher than an eagle,
'cause you are the wind beneath my wings.

(continued...)

It is doubtful that the narrators would have shared their intimate stories if they were much younger. On one hand, at this stage of their lives, those who are most likely to criticize them are not around anymore. Several are well established that they could care less even if they are criticized.

CONTACT INFORMATION

The narrators could be contacted via the following email:

TwoScore.4YearsAgo@gmail.com

The list of musical URLs or links can also be requested via this email address.

REFERENCES

This book is intended to be used along with the materials, below. These were particularly selected due to the Diaspora component of growing up.

- THE IMMIGRANT ADVANTAGE - by Claudia Kolker

  What Immigrants Can Teach the Rest of America

  http://www.youtube.com/watch?v=31BWtTekc8Y
  http://www.youtube.com/watch?v=gW76KhA1OJk

  The Immigrant advantage

  http://www.youtube.com/watch?v=FqCW73ZA4tw

  Houston's Immigrant Advantage (Complete)

  http://www.youtube.com/watch?v=DGF4lq8bWRw

  Outline from Immigrant Advantage

  - How to Save: Vietnamese Money Club
  - How to Mother a Mother: Mexican Cuarentana
  - How to Court: South Asian Assisted Marriage
  - How to Learn: Korean and Chinese Afterschools
  - How to Shelter: West Indian Multi-generational Households
  - How to be A good Neighbor: Barrio Stoops, Sidewalks and Shops
  - How to Eat: Vietnamese Monthly Rice
  - How to Collect: The American Money Club
  - How to Perform Community Service: Ibo Ogbo

- JOB MARKET: SURVIVAL GUIDE 2012 AND BEYOND

- Plutarch - Lucius Mestrius Plutarchus (46 – 120 AD)

  http://en.wikipedia.org/wiki/Plutarch

- Josephus - Titus Flavius Josephus (37 – c. 100)] aka Joseph Ben Matityahu

  http://en.wikipedia.org/wiki/Josephus

FOOD FOR THOUGHT

THE PARADOX OF OUR TIME – attributed to George Carlin (recipient of the Mark Twain Prize for American Humor) upon the death of his wife.

The paradox of our time in history is that we have taller buildings but shorter tempers, wider Freeways , but narrower viewpoints. We spend more, but have less, we buy more, but enjoy less. We have bigger houses and smaller families, more conveniences, but less time. We have more degrees but less sense, more knowledge, but less judgment, more experts, yet more problems, more medicine, but less wellness.

We drink too much, smoke too much, spend too recklessly, laugh too little, drive too fast, get too angry, stay up too late, get up too tired, read too little, watch TV too much, and pray too seldom.

We have multiplied our possessions, but reduced our values. We talk too much, love too seldom, and hate too often.

We've learned how to make a living, but not a life. We've added years to life not life to years. We've been all the way to the moon and back, but have trouble crossing the street to meet a new neighbor. We conquered outer space but not inner space. We've done larger things, but not better things.

We've cleaned up the air, but polluted the soul. We've conquered the atom, but not our prejudice. We write more, but learn less. We plan more, but accomplish less. We've learned to rush, but not to wait. We build more computers to hold more information, to produce more copies than ever, but we communicate less and less.

These are the times of fast foods and slow digestion, big men and small character, steep profits and shallow relationships. These are the days of two incomes but more divorce, fancier houses, but broken homes. These are days of quick trips, disposable diapers, throwaway morality, one night stands, overweight bodies, and pills that do everything from cheer, to quiet, to kill. It is a time when there is much in the showroom window and nothing in the stockroom. A time when technology can bring this letter to you, and a time when you can choose either to share this insight, or to just hit delete...

Remember; spend some time with your loved ones, because they are not going to be around forever.

Remember, say a kind word to someone who looks up to you in awe, because that little person soon will grow up and leave your side.

Remember, to give a warm hug to the one next to you, because that is the only treasure you can give with your heart and it doesn't cost a cent.

Remember, to say, 'I love you' to your partner and your loved ones, but most of all mean it. A kiss and an embrace will mend hurt when it comes from deep inside of you.

Remember to hold hands and cherish the moment for someday that person will not be there again.

Give time to love, give time to speak! And give time to share the precious thoughts in your mind.

AND ALWAYS REMEMBER:

Life is not measured by the number of breaths we take, but by the moments that take our breath away.

1000 MARBLES – Author: Unknown

http://moneyover55.about.com/od/managingdebt/a/1000marbles.htm

The older I get, the more I enjoy Saturday mornings. Perhaps it's the quiet solitude that comes with being the first to rise, or maybe it's the unbounded joy of not having to be at work. Either way, the first few hours of a Saturday morning are most enjoyable.

A few weeks ago, I was shuffling toward the backyard patio with a steaming cup of coffee in one hand and the morning paper in the other. What began as a typical Saturday morning, turned into one of those lessons that life seems to hand you from time to time. Let me tell you about it.

I turned the dial up to listen to a Saturday morning talk show I heard an older sounding gentleman, with a golden voice. You know the kind, he sounded like he should be in the broadcasting business. He was telling whoever he was talking with something about "a thousand marbles".

I was intrigued and stopped to listen to what he had to say...

"Well, Tom, it sure sounds like you're busy with your job. I'm sure they pay you well but it's a shame you have to be away from home and your family so much. Hard to believe a young fellow should have to work sixty or seventy hours a week to make ends meet. Too bad you missed your daughter's dance recital."

He continued, "Let me tell you something Tom, something that has helped me keep a good perspective on my own priorities."

And that's when he began to explain his theory of a "thousand marbles." "You see, I sat down one day and did a little arithmetic. The average person lives about seventy-five years. I know, some live more and some live less, but on average, folks live about seventy-five years."

"Now then, I multiplied 75 times 52 and I came up with 3900 which is the number of Saturdays that the average person has in their entire lifetime.

Now stick with me Tom, I'm getting to the important part."

"It took me until I was fifty-five years old to think about all this in any detail", he went on, "and by that time I had lived through over twenty-eight hundred Saturdays. I got to thinking that if I lived to be seventy-five, I only had about a thousand of them left to enjoy."

"So I went to a toy store and bought every single marble they had. I ended up having to visit three toy stores to round-up 1000 marbles. I took them home and put them inside of a large, clear plastic container right here in the shack next to my gear. Every Saturday since then, I have taken one marble out and thrown it away."

"I found that by watching the marbles diminish, I focused more on the really important things in life. There is nothing like watching your time here on this earth run out to help get your priorities straight."

"Now let me tell you one last thing before I sign-off with you and take my lovely wife out for breakfast. This morning, I took the very last marble out of the container. I figure if I make it until next Saturday then I have been given a little extra time. And the one thing we can all use is a little more time."

"It was nice to meet you Tom, I hope you spend more time with your family, and I hope to meet you again.

You could have heard a pin drop on the radio when this fellow signed off. I guess he gave us all a lot to think about. I had planned to work that morning.

Instead, I went upstairs and woke my wife up with a kiss. "C'mon honey, I'm taking you and the kids to breakfast."

"What brought this on?" she asked with a smile. "Oh, nothing special, it's just been a while since we spent a Saturday together with the kids. Hey, can we stop at a toy store while we're out? I need to buy some marbles."

The Farmer's Son (Bank Business Manager)

Being one of the Go-To persons for the UECHS-69 Alumni group, it is a privilege and honor to share a narrative that in one form or another is a fusion of various adversities, challenges, opportunities, values and connection that have been made possible, facilitated and nurtured, directly or indirectly, through UECHS, its administration and staff, faculty, students and alumni groups.

Compared to most of you, my narrative might not be a typical story, and if you will bear with me, I am hoping that you will find out why. Briefly, I did not have a childhood and any level of normalcy that most individuals are blessed with but take for granted.

THE EARLY YEARS

I came from a family of hard working and struggling farmers in a remote area of Masbate. My father was originally from Cebu, and my mother was originally from Bohol. Although I started school at the age of 6-1/2 years, the hard life, the need to assist my father in the farm, and to perform various chores, frequently interrupted and delayed my studies.

The family's resources were insufficient to support my education beyond elementary grade 4. Education being very important to me as early as I could remember, and given the harsh reality of the situation, I asked my father to allow me to explore the world on my own. I believe in the saying "That everyone has its own destiny, and it is imperative to follow it, accept it, no matter what may come". "Follow your own star." – Dante Alighieri (http://en.wikipedia.org/wiki/Dante_Alighieri).

When my father heard this, tears poured from his eyes, and he pleaded with me to stay. He was probably happy knowing that education would allow me to escape the tyranny and curse of hardship, but on the other hand, the price of that promise was losing me. He bought a sewing machine for me so I could study tailoring. I studied tailoring, and after three months I knew enough to sew a polo and trouser on my own. However, weak lungs stopped me from continuing with sewing, but this skill will help me later in life.

Life was extremely difficult and trying during these times. Besides farming, I had to handle dry goods marketing which required frequent walking up to 21 kilometers with the merchandize carried on horseback to catch up with the market day in some distant place, and a ride on a motor boat to peddle the goods.

ARRIVED IN MANILA

At the age of 18, a business accident and an internal conspiracy required me to leave Masbate in haste. I arrived in Manila with only 2 pairs of clothing, a pair of rubber shoes and 2.00 Pesos in my pocket. This sudden and unplanned separation from the family and friends was one of those challenges that I had to live with.

I first landed in Nepomuceno Street, Tondo Manila where I was employed as a helper in cleaning pigpens, feeding the pigs, and in preparing the pigs for delivery to slaughterhouses. It was hard work capturing & tying the pigs, then weighing them in the weight scales, then untying them again. The work is routine and at the end of the day, I was dead tired. I worked there for three months, and decided to look for lighter job, and boy did I find one!

I landed a job in a dormitory where we prepared food for female student boarders. I thought I found an easy work assisting the cook in food preparation, not knowing that we had to clean the entire dormitory as well. Several female boarders tried to seduce me – ala Mrs. Robinson style in the "Graduate" - http://en.wikipedia.org/wiki/The_Graduate . While cleaning their rooms, they would lie on bed with their revealing underwears while talking and staring at me.

In terms of work, I would go to sleep at past 12 midnight and wake up to start working at 4 am - everyday.

Since fooling around was not a priority, and returning to school was, and before I get into trouble, I decided to return to Masbate.

BACK TO MASBATE

This time, I was introduced to a shipper of livestock from Masbate to Manila. He was the one who provided me with the opportunity to work under his wing, while concurrently studying at UECHS.

The daily routine in Masbate included: purchasing livestock in rural areas; cashiering; preparing livestock for transport; and, transporting livestock to ships including climbing stairs made of double 2x4 board 10 meters long with 45 degrees from the ground up to the ship deck with live, shrieking and struggling pigs on my shoulder, and if I ever slipped and fell, I would land on a concrete floor, or in the water (the latter being the preferred landing of choice).

BACK TO MANILA

After 2 years, this shipper eventually entrusted me with overseeing all the shipment of livestock's delivered to different slaughterhouses in the Metro Manila area, including Vitas in Tondo, FTI in Taguig, Marulas in Valenzuela and Caloocan City. I stayed in Caloocan City to consolidate the proceeds of the shipment and transfer it back to Masbate thru the facilities of Philippine National Bank (PNB).

THE UECHS DAYS

I was a 20 year old in a class of mostly high school freshmen 13-14 year olds and a few 18-19 olds. My daily routine was: sleep at 7pm, wake up at 12am; reported to work at 1am; worked from 1am to 9am; then went to school between 10am to 5pm. This hectic schedule provided no time for studying off-campus, or participating in any extra-curricular activities.

On certain days when live-stocks arrive, I would work double time, and be awake for 48 consecutive hours without sleeping. I am accountable to all workers, including loading and unloading live-stocks, preparing bill of ladings, paying obligations and expenses, etc.

My biggest challenge from freshman through senior years at that time was keeping awake while the class was taking place, and lack of money. But the UE instructors, aware of my situation, were very considerate and forgiving.

In second year, I was elected class president. I met RM and we became intimate secretly lasting into 1st year in college.

In the third and fourth years, I remained class president.

THE BULLIES

Working and studying concurrently involved different challenges and dynamics. Due to limited budget, I walked from my place of residence to UE Caloocan, Samson Road across a railroad.

One time while walking along the railway, I passed by several naughty boys, and one of them strucked me from behind. When I faced them, they threw stones at me, but a railway guard stopped them. I reported the incident to the police, and I was not disturbed from that point on.

My first day in college was a horrible day. I was a holdup victim. Several men forcibly led me into a small street where they took my wallet and watch. During that ordeal, I had to think of dropping my ambition. My strong faith in GOD prevailed. I thank HIM for keeping from harm.

THE LOVES OF MY LIFE

I lost my first love in Masbate because my priority was education and I had to leave in haste.

While living in Caloocan and taking my high school at UECHS, I was seduced by, and had a relationship with an older woman.

Then I met RM and had a relationship with her from second year high school to 1st year college.

I lost RM to a businessman due to pressure from her father.

Then I met Mildred R, and we got married in 1974.

I could best articulate my thoughts and feelings through the musical pieces below. Even now, I bore the lasting trauma of these losses and tragedies. Keep in mind that I have been deprived of childhood and various normalcies that most individuals take for granted.

I HAVE WHO HAVE NOTHING – TOM JONES

http://www.youtube.com/watch?v=9rgLd6A0DWM

THE IMPOSSIBLE DREAM – LUTHER VANDROSS

http://www.youtube.com/watch?v=AijRBQf-ato

YOU'LL NEVER WALK ALONE – TOM JONES

http://www.youtube.com/watch?v=dSeZdqSsyRI

NO MAN IS AN ISLAND – THE LETTERMEN

http://www.youtube.com/watch?v=hWlMfmsIW8U

MEMORIES – BARBARA STREISAND

http://www.youtube.com/watch?v=n-KPGh3wysw

MEMORIES – CATS

http://www.youtube.com/watch?v=4-L6rEm0rnY

I DREAMED A DREAM – ANNA HATHAWAY & HAYLE WESTENRA

http://www.youtube.com/watch?v=SyQ-0JOF1Qk
http://www.youtube.com/watch?v=ZSwx2MdUKzw
http://www.youtube.com/watch?v=7JP3AVGW9hM

AMAZING GRACE – HAYLE WESTENRA

http://www.youtube.com/watch?v=5mnTKN8LuiY

WHEN I FALL IN LOVE – LETTERMEN & NAT KING COLE

http://www.youtube.com/watch?v=Dq4PDKDsW-s
http://www.youtube.com/watch?v=GfAb0gNPy6s

THE FIRST TIME I SAW YOUR FACE – ROBERTA FLACK

http://www.youtube.com/watch?v=hOFrGbuUqnQ

KILLING ME SOFTLY WITH HIS SONG – ROBERTA FLACK

http://www.youtube.com/watch?v=LQ2t5e7stVM

WE SHALL OVERCOME

http://www.youtube.com/watch?v=RkNsEH1GD7Q

ROLE OF UECHS TO MY PERSONAL, FAMILY AND PROFESSIONAL CAREER

UECHS welcomed me, and provided a home when I desperately needed one. UECHS accepted me for what I am, and not what I should be. What I had become, and what I am today is a fusion of the adversities, challenges, opportunities, values and connection that have been made possible, facilitated and nurtured, directly or indirectly, through UECHS, its administration and staff, faculty, students and alumni groups.

Because of UECHS and my early experience, at PNB I was assigned and promoted to the following positions: bookkeeper; Credit Investigator; Appraiser; Accountant; Cashier; Loan Officer; finally, Business Manager before retiring. I supplemented my earnings by sewing which I learned in the early days in Masbate.

The lyrics of the song below, guided my personal and professional approach to life.

No Man is an Island

http://www.youtube.com/watch?v=hWlMfmsIW8U

No man is an island,
No man stands alone,
Each man's joy is joy to me,
Each man's grief is my own.

We need one another,
So I will defend,
Each man as my brother,
Each man as my friend.

I saw the people gather,
I heard the music start,
The song that they were singing,
Is ringing in my heart.

No man is an island,
Way out in the blue,
We all look to the one above,
For our strength to renew.

When I help my brother,
Then I know that I,
Plant the seed of friendship,
That will never die.

(continued...)

LOOKING BACK

The fighting spirit and perseverance coupled with God fearing inspiration allowed me to be where I am today. During the early days, I only dreamed of being able to go to Manila, and acquire a college degree. I never expected that I would be able to reach America, China and South Africa. Who could have imagined that a son of a humble and struggling farmer could have reached these places?

I am a living model of how a son of a humble and struggling farmer could make it in society.

With Love for the People and my Country...

- The Farmer's Son (Bank Business Manager)

The Office Wife (Administrative Assistant to the Director, School of Medicine, University of California, San Francisco)

Just I love You and Goodbye...
36 months, and 7 days ago

IN 2010

That's about how long you've been gone. All this time I've been praying and hoping that if you could, even for once, talk to me in my dreams. Through our past times, we've done many things together. Now, I have had to move on with my life into greater things. I knew that this day would come; I could see it coming around the corner. My expectation of what things would be like was above what has actually become I want things to be the way they used to be... Talking all the time, laughing for no apparent reason, all of these memories, I know I will carry them always in my heart. I can go back and play them over again in my head, so make it seem as though everything is the way it used to be. If I could, I would build a time machine and replay all of the wonderful times that we have had together. I don't want to know what it would be like losing my best friend but not realizing that I have already loss my best friend and my loving husband.

IN 2009

One day in September, you left early to go to work and you said you are not coming home for lunch because you have a doctor's appointment. I was surprised seeing you sad and tears coming down from your eyes and you said that you had cancer. How could there be pain in a place where there is so much joy? A loving relationship is the most awesome experience in the world. This is why it also holds the potential for so much sadness. So many things can go wrong. Not once did I expect this to happen. I can't imagine even in my wildest dream that I will be losing you before your 60th birthday. I was holding you in my arms, waking you up, asking you to open up your eyes but you did not move. Oh my God, I saw Ronel, your one and only son that you've loved so much sobbing, crying. Why, oh why did you stop breathing, why you left us suddenly not even saying goodbye. I was crying until there are no more tears. I can't help but think about...

ALL ALONE AM I – Brenda Lee

http://www.youtube.com/watch?v=wnApJcGBDFY

"All alone am I
Ever since your goodbye

27

All alone with just a beat of my heart
People all around
However, I don't hear a sound
Just the lonely beating of my heart"

(continued...)

I thought my sadness and loneliness will stop from here but no, your good old buddy "nanay" followed were you are "Safely Home" both of my dear ones are in heaven. However, I'm still alone because our son was deployed for the third time and I'm happy to let you know that his beautiful girlfriend together with her two siblings stayed with me to keep me company.

I wonder, is it all possible to learn the harsh lessons of our life? Indeed, in most social spheres we can hope to consider our previous mistakes and avoid in the future. Confusion over this question constitutes the kaleidoscope of my memory of my high school days at the University of the East-Caloocan High School (UECHS).

AGE: 12-16

I was 12 years old when I enrolled at UECHS and at this age of mine, my primary goal was to finish high school so that I could better myself in the future. I did not expect my high school days would be dull, unexciting and routine. I joined the UECHS dance group, made it good in class and kept on smiling to all classmates/schoolmates but still no one paid attention to me. I was hoping that someone would ask me to the junior/senior prom, but not a single soul invited me to be his dance partner. Its graduation, a parental dream, a day supposed to be the happiest at least in a half a decade, exciting, emotional, saying final goodbyes and tears swelling in my eyes. I am very excited one of my classmates introduced to me to his friend and was hoping he will invite me to the graduation party. Unfortunately, my hope was in vain. I went home feeling sorry for my mom who had bought two dresses for me to wear, one for the graduation and one for the party. Before leaving the campus, four of my professors approached and congratulated me for a job well done. I was so happy and excited because now am proud of myself even with the unkind campus environment. School has made me bright I could no longer hesitate and to obtain more education in college.

AGE: 16-21

UE Manila was where I decided to attend college. I took typing and stenography and pursue my major which is accounting and management. While in school, I was able to work at several government agencies, private companies and hotels. I had been involved also with school/class activities, which helped me overcome my weakness. I had more friends now than in high school because I became more articulate and outgoing due to the fact the kind of work I was doing, in and out of school. One of my HS friends became one of my classmate and we started dating. I was on "Top of the

World", was the love that I've found every since he's been around... In addition, most of my professors became my friends that help me to accomplish my goals and they gave me valuable advice. It made me think that if in HS I was chatty and unreserved; probably my HS days would be more enjoyable. However, it's not too late, after 44 years not seeing my classmates and batch mates, the Las Vegas reunion last June 2013 was fun, entertaining and delightful seeing familiar faces once again. It's just like "Don't worry, be happy".

AGE: 28-61

In January 1980, two of my sisters and I migrated to U.S and deep in my heart, I know it's going to be a period of adjustment just like high school. Looking for a job in the Bay Area was not easy. I started as a clerk for the Deaf and Blind Association, telex operator at CTI and hotel supervisor at Holiday Inn. Having local experience, applied as a clerk at the University of California, San Francisco and worked my way up as an administrative assistant to the Director of our department under the School of Medicine. The only Filipina in our department, my life was a struggle. Fortunately, my first supervisor lived in the Philippines for 3 years and said that Filipinos are hard worker. I was given multiple tasks and was able to complete these tasks ahead of time and my position was classified and re-classified but was not given a chance to be promoted on a managerial level because of my orientation. With my ethnic background, the price of success is hard work and dedication to the job and the determination to be successful was best applied at hand to us to the task. I was handling 3 Hypertension Satellite clinics, grants submission to NIH, NDC and Private Corporation, FDA and CHR protocols, evaluations of nurses, residents, lab techs and dietary personnel and at the same time assisting in procuring medical journals and books for submission of articles and book chapters to different medical societies. I've handled all my responsibilities with less supervision while being a mom, wife and a daughter. Eventually, my hard work and dedication comes with a price, I got too sick to go to work and have to undergo different types of therapies and surgeries. After years of therapies and treatments, it's time to quit my job to continue the healing process.

The struggle of my life creates empathy, I could relate to pain, being ignored and people not loving me. Always remember that striving and struggle precede success and without a struggle, there can be no progress.

Now that time has passed, I of course will remember the emotional uneasiness that accompanied me after high school days and the passing of my loved ones. These had a huge impact on my life- for the better. However, while being perhaps less naive now, I am no longer too pessimistic. Yes, it is a daunting task to learn all lessons of our life because we tend to forget them. Nevertheless, if leaves a trace of our emotional experiences, then probably we can overcome the arguments without the principal solution. Well, this is exactly what I have tried to do; I believe that it is necessary to turn our experiences into words that represent them as close as possible, so that others and we could relive them upon reading.

If given a chance to be in high school again, I will be more friendly, I will not stress, I will be patient, I will try new sports and activities, and really explore who we are as individuals. I know how hard things can seem in high school, but they will all pass.

The memory of past is like a rainbow, bright, vivid, and beautiful; but it soon fades away.

Just like one of Barry Manilow's song, **"I made it through the rain:"**

http://www.youtube.com/watch?v=Gr0LHm4SgEA
http://www.youtube.com/watch?v=AqApdSxbwak

We dreamers have our ways
Of facing rainy days
And somehow we survive
We keep the feelings warm
Protect them from the storm
Until our time arrives
Then one day the sun appears
And we come shining through those lonely years
I made it through the rain
I kept my world protected
I made it through the rain
I kept my point of view
I made it through the rain
And found myself respected
By the others who
Got rained on too
And made it through
When friends are hard to find
And life seems so unkind
Sometimes you feel afraid
Just aim beyond the clouds
And rise above the crowds
And start your own parade
'Cause when I chased my fears away
That's when I knew that I could finally say
I made it through the rain
I kept my world protected

(continued...)

- The Office Wife (Administrative Assistant to the Director, School of

30

Medicine, University of California, San Francisco)

The Zumba Girl (Nurse at Kaiser Permanente)

My University of the East-Caloocan High School (UECHS) experience was the most memorable stage of my life. It was a time of innocence, confusing events, and longing for acceptance in the social structure.

My priorities during high school were: (1) acceptance by friends, (2) watching boys, and, (3) oh well academics.

I found the very best friends in high school, we had a wonderful and endearing relationship. Life was difficult with so many "boy crushes", so many to keep my eyes on, oh my…..my head was spinning, lots of cute boys in high school. I got nervous/shaky every time I see "them", my heart was pounding….unfortunately and sadly, none of them even bothered to wink at me. Tears on my pillow …You don't remember me, but I remember you, it was not that long ago, you broke my heart in two. Tears on my pillow, pain in my heart, all caused by you!

It was so funny because my crush didn't even know that I liked him so much.
One time, one of the girls in the class made a scrap book that she passed around to answer all kinds of personal questions like "who is your crush", etc. I was so excited to go through all the names who signed it. When I saw that I was not the chosen one by this cute crush of mine…..huhuhuhu….again tears on my pillows. Hahahahaha too funny to think about it now, many years later.

Then graduation came, everyone bid good bye to each other. Sad to say that for me that was the last contact with everyone.

AGE: 16-21

The second chapter of my life was the transition from high school to college. It was a life with lots of challenges requiring plenty of adjustments. But it was also exciting and promising because of freedom and the transition to adulthood. Life in college was a roller coaster, sad times, and fun times.

My first days of college was a nightmare, always wondering what the professors would be expecting of us, how to approach other students coming from various provinces. They were smart, beautiful and intimidating. College was exhausting. I spent memorable days and nights in the library, in my bedroom studying, memorizing, tons of homework and projects to complete, and deadlines to meet. I hated all these work, but I did them anyway, hoping that someday it will be all worth it.

There went my dream of freedom, I was again a prisoner of all these work.
But, I said to myself, this is fine. This is building the foundation of who I am, and who I would be. Thou I felt like imprisoned in college, I met very interesting friends whom I am still in contact here in the US.

We had good memories, such as the picnics at different beaches in the outskirt of Manila, the overnight beach parties during summer breaks, and attending fiestas at my barkadas' provinces. It was so much fun during school breaks.

College ended and just the song by the Carpenters that goes like this:

WE'VE ONLY JUST BEGAN - CARPENTERS

http://www.youtube.com/watch?v=__VQX2Xn7tI

We've only just begun to live
White lace and promises
A kiss for luck and we're on our way
We've only begun

Before the risin' sun, we fly
So many roads to choose
We'll start out walkin' and learn to run
And yes, we've just begun.......

(continued...)

AGE: 22-43

The third chapter of my life was the best moment of my life. I migrated to the United States, this is where Life began.

Just a short background from my personal life, I got married but then divorced after 20 years of blissful marriage to a navy man. We had a daughter who is a teacher and 3 grandchildren whom I love so much.

I found out that life in a new country came with its own set of challenges. I had to deal with realities like finding a job, looking for suitable housing because living with the in- laws, which was not fun at all, and being accustomed to the culture.

Finding a job, related to your course was impossible during the late 1970's. Just to get out of the in laws' house, I started working in the supermarket, worked at the pen maker assembly line. The Pinoy pride was negatively creeping in. But thank God, based on the advice of new friends, they made me accept the fact that this is part of transitioning here in the United States, particularly if you came from another culture.

So I swallowed the Pinoy pride, I did not let it stand in the way of pursuing a different path of life, and worked very hard in achieving my goals.

Then came the housing from the military. Most of our furniture were donated by the navy. This was a moment of happiness because we are on our own, away from the in-laws.

Then pregnancy came. I had my daughter. I quit work, took care of the baby and the hubby full time. Being married to a military person was a challenge as well. I am alone most of the time, alone raising our child, alone in making all the decisions in life. This is a battle for survival.

There were lots of lonely days , the thought of being away from my Mom, Dad and my brothers ... was hard, even thou I have my own family, my husband (ex) and my wonderful daughter, I still missed my parents, siblings, friends and relatives especially on holiday, I was homesick a lot.

Thou I met good people from different types and at various status levels, old friends and families are still the best company.

I had lots of sacrifices and sad days.

When my daughter started grade school, I was again on the work force. Luckily, I landed a job at a major bottling company at the Information system department, a good job that gave us a good start in life, we were able to buy a our first home, then moved to a bigger home, and then again to a bigger home. But divorce destroyed all that we built together.
I lost my job at the bottling company because of the merger and automation.

AGE: 44-48

I decided to work in the insurance department of a medical facility. Then I had the opportunity to transfer to and work at the Internal Medicine as the person who assigned Physicians from every floor, from ER to every ward and floors in the hospital 24 X 7.
It was a tough and challenging job, but very rewarding.
The hospital I worked for provided the opportunity to send 10 qualified employees to go to a nursing school. Being a healthcare professional was not my original career choice. I was a Fine Arts graduate. But I applied anyway. Out of 300 applicants, I passed the required exams and extensive panel interviews. Those selected were provided tuition free, given only 2 days to work, and got paid full time. I had to go to school for 4 days and nights - lectures during the day, clinicals were at night and on weekends.

AGE: 49-51

Going to school at later age was the most stressful part of my life. I found out that education here in US and the Philippines were totally different. The education in the U.S. focuses on critical thinking, and less on rote memory.

While taking nursing, I had no life at all, no friends, not much of family association either, no television, my music was my taped lecture from the class, no eating out, no socialization for two years. There were plenty of sacrifices.

AGE: 52-61

I wish I took nursing when I was younger. I wish I had a mentor or a counselor to guide and hold my hand to better career choices that provide long-term opportunities.

I can't complain now that I am in my 60s. I am a lot wiser now. All these adversities and challenges built my character, and made me a better person. Being in health care, provided me with the opportunity to providing service and making a difference on the lives of patients, their families and loved ones – at their most vulnerable and critical moments.

My advice to all, especially my loved ones, my grandkids, nieces and nephews, is to seek and acquire a good and solid education. Identify life-long mentors who will guide you. Keep a balance between time with family, friends, work and leisure time. Recognize your strengths and weaknesses and surround yourself with the right people.

Set goals and priorities, develop a plan and execute a plan of action.

Whatever you/they chose in life, be strong, never give up, and don't let failure stop or slow you down. Always aim for the best and aim high. Be financially independent. Don't forget to be a good person.

I thank my Grandchildren for loving their Nana, to my daughter Jennifer, My Mom and much love to my Father (deceased), my brothers and their families, my Ex who showed me and taught me to be a woman, my friends and classmates and to my Woody who gave their wholehearted support . You are all my inspirations in life.

I would like to thank David Paraiso for encouraging me to write this narrative. After writing my life experiences, I realized that my life was on the fast lane. Whoaaa I did all these????? What a trip!

I would like to share this inspirational quote from an anonymous source:

> In life there are going to be obstacles that will cause interference,
> but we must learn to overcome these challenges and grow stronger.

In life there are fears that will hold us back from what we want,
but we must learn to fight them with the courage from within.

LOOKING BACK

Given a second chance to be a 12-16 year-old again, I would seek out mentor(s) who will assist and guide me in defining, planning and executing professional & personal goals. Because I did not have any, I did not take high school that seriously, I was ill equipped in facing adversities and challenges, and I landed a stable career late in life.

-   The Zumba Girl (Nurse at Kaiser Permanente)

The Good Daughter from North Carolina (Accountant)

THE GOOD DAUGHTER, THE DREAMER and THE BELIEVER.........

My high school years laid a foundation for me to pursue a higher degree. The knowledge I gained in high school made my college life a little bit easier. I consider myself lucky to be surrounded by some of the smartest and brightest students. Although I felt that I could not catch up with them, I was inspired and challenged to push my capacity to work harder to better myself for the future. I loved interacting with them. They were so smart that just being with them made me feel important for welcoming me into their group.

Did anyone of you have a clear vision then of who and what you will be in forty four years? If you do, CONGRATULATIONS! I did not. What happened between now and high school is in its own story if not an entire book since it had been over four decades ago since we graduated. Some of us have had our share of broken relationships, career drifts and disappointments, joys and victories.
High school was a learning experience and it was a turning point in my life. It helped me mature as a person both mentally and emotionally. They were four years I will always cherish and would never trade for anything.

NO ONE ELSE WILL SHAPE A DREAM INTO REALITY BUT YOU!

Today's generations seems to have it better; modern technology for one. Although it speeds up the process, the critical thinking is still needed to process information that cannot be learned by on-line surfing. So, what can I share with the next generations of high schoolers? - Know what you are good at and what you want. - Plan your careers and focus, do not allow obstacles to deter you from your goals. - Learn from your mistakes and defeats and do not allow frustrations and disappointments to ruin your life. - Try to do your best and regret nothing if it did not turn out the way you wanted it to be. - Get involved in school activities and maintain a good relationship with those around you. - Make good use of the resources that are now available to you. - Believe in yourself. Your time now is a more complex and challenging world than ours. There is a lot to learn but try to grow from the challenge and never lose sight of who you are. Always remember that problems are meant to be solved. Do not be afraid because they will enhance your personal experience. - Be proactive so that when adversities come your way, you are ready. Everybody is given the same opportunity to rise beyond what is expected.

University of the East-Caloocan High School (UECHS) was my school of choice even before I finished elementary school. It was closer to home for one and also because I had heard about the teachers who are truly committed to students' learning. My high school days were some of the best years of my life. I got to meet students that shared some of my same interests and some who made a positive difference on how I learned about life. All my high school years I only had female classmates. So there was very little interaction with male classmates. I got to see them only during recess time or school activities outside of class. I would shy away most of the time whenever they were close by. You see, I was a shy girl growing up in a tight-knit family and was sheltered from a lot of things that other girls my age were into. I was also a little insecure and timid around people I did not know. I often admired those who were outspoken and talkative – they usually stood out. *"Could it be because they did not care what others thought of them?"* I realized now that this is somewhat a good quality to have since more often than not, insecurity can break a person. So, if only I knew then what I know now, I would have participated more on the after school activities in order to bring out my *"potential"* I knew I had.

YEAR OF INNOCENCE!

High school was also the time when I learned what it meant to be promiscuous. One memory that stood out among others was one that seemed funny to me now but so new to me then. It started out so innocently. Our school required girls to wear a blue skirt, white blouse and blue vest as our uniform. And so, at the beginning of each class, our white blouse had to be tucked in and our blue vest could be open or closed. There was this one incident in our class where I still vividly remember a certain classmate who skipped class to be with her boyfriend. And every time she skipped class and came back, her blouse was in disarray. One day, one of our classmates asked me, *"Did you notice her blouse?"* And I replied, *"What is wrong with her blouse?"* She laughed at me. Two other classmates who happened to be whispering and listening also joined her. From this snickering and whispering in regards to her behavior, I learned a few life lessons about the birds and the bees. *That shows you how naïve I was back then*.

Another life experience on trying to figure out what I wanted my career to be after high school graduation was determined when I participated in our school Red Cross blood drive. I was so excited to be given the task of assisting one of the nurses. But upon seeing the blood come through the tube, I passed out. **Whew!** At that point I knew nursing was not for me!

Music was also part of my everyday life. I remember singing in class a lot of times with one of our classmates, Marilou Cortez. She had one of the most beautiful voices in our class, and there were times I would wish that I had the same gift. In fact, I was looking forward to meeting her at the past reunion in Las Vegas so I could hear her sing again, but she was not able to make it. I love singing so much and dreamed of pursuing it if given the chance. Unfortunately now, I cannot sing anymore as my vocal chords were affected when I had a total thyroid removal over 7 years ago. *So, there goes seeing one of my dreams go down the drain!*

I also met my best friend, the Doctor from Yorba Linda. We shared the same passion for music among other things. Almost every afternoon I would be at her house with Hermie Chua, and he would play the piano, and the three of us would sing.

AGE: 16-20
A GREAT STORY ABOUT MY LIFE.....TO BE OR NOT TO BE!

When I enrolled in college, I wanted to take Physical Education (PE) because swimming was one of the sports that had to be taken in order to get a passing grade. As far as I can remember, I always wanted to swim but never learned how to because I was always afraid of the water. I almost drowned when I was younger, and that was a very frightening and traumatic experience. Unfortunately, I didn't have the nerve to do it, so to spare myself from embarrassment I looked for another option besides PE. I ended up enrolling in WATC, also known as Women's Auxiliary Training Corps. This was similar to ROTC for males. It was so much fun especially because our company commander was very nice to me. I became the envy of the group. I did not realize then that she was a lesbian and that she had developed very special feelings for me. **"Hmmm",** I said to myself, shall I reciprocate so that I can continue the luxury of being treated well or face her wrath later on. Luckily, fate decided it for me. Had it not been for a welcome intervention then, I would have probably given in and turned into someone like herself. You see, we were invited to spend our school break over at the assistant company commander's home in *Candaba, Pampanga*. Originally, the plan was our company commander would be coming with us, along with four other officers, but she cancelled at the last minute. She was heartbroken and begged me to stay, but I insisted that I wanted to join the group. **"It was a life-changing decision!"**

We were all so excited that day when we were waiting for the bus that would take us to Pampanga. *Especially so* for me since that was my very first time to be away from home and I just turned 19. **"Imagine that!"** We were all seated at the back of the bus talking and laughing when suddenly one of them said, *"Why don't you sing a song for us Picaña"*. Somehow, Picaña seems to be easier to say than my first name Eufranda. Anyway, back to the story. The rest of the group stopped talking and all said almost instantaneously, *"Come on Picaña, sing a song for us, sing a song for us please"*. Being a good sport and all, I obliged. For some unknown reason, the first song that came to mind was a **love song** because I just happened to like the melody and I want to share with you the lyrics to that song……

Where is love?

http://www.youtube.com/watch?v=WjJDekSculo

> *Where is love?*
> *Does it fall from skies above?*
> *Is it underneath the willow tree*
> *That I've been dreaming of?*
> *Where is she?*
> *Who I close my eyes to see?*
> *Will I ever know the sweet "hello"*
> *That's only meant for me?*
> *Who can say where she may hide?*
> *Must I travel far and wide?*
> *'Til I am beside that someone who I can mean something to ...*

(continued...)

LITTLE DID I KNOW THAT MY LIFE WAS NOT GOING TO BE THE SAME AFTER THAT SONG!

It was *November 1970*, around 2:30 p.m. The temperature was in the 80s. The memory of that day when the assistant commander introduced us to this wonderful, good looking guy, who was also her childhood friend, is still very fresh in my mind as if it just happened today. He was also there on a school break to celebrate their town fiesta. **"Boy, oh boy,"** I thought I was in a trance. I must say whatever I felt that day was so new to me. I didn't want that memorable afternoon to end. My heart was beating so fast, especially when he told us that he was swinging by her house in the evening to get to know us better. Being so shy and so naïve at that time, I did not even say one word when we were being formally introduced. I had no idea at the time that I caught his attention because of that. Mind you, I felt the other four girls were prettier so it never crossed my mind that he even thought of me, let alone being interested in me.

Guess what – Remember that wonderful, good looking guy I met at the town fiesta? He ended up being my husband, and we are still together after **36 ½ years** through ups and downs.

AGE: 21-26
CHALLENGES AND PERSEVERANCE

After my college graduation in 1973 from the University of the East, Manila, I started my professional career at the Phoenix Press, Inc. in Quezon City. After working for nearly a year as an accountant, I was ready to take on more responsibility, but the growth was not there at the time. As much as I loved living in the Philippines with my family and friends, I had to go abroad to pursue better opportunities. So, with a heavy heart, I left for London, England in 1973. It was not easy being away from my loved ones.

My father's income was no longer sufficient enough for us so I had to do whatever was necessary to help him provide for our family. Before I left for London, England, my only sister, who was eleven years old at that time asked me so innocently, **"Ate, bakit aalis ka pa?"** (Why do you have to leave, elder sister?) With teary eyes, I answered, **"Kasi para matulungan kitang makatapos ng pag aaral. (so that I can help you complete your schooling)"** With that promise to her and to my other two younger brothers that I will help them achieve their dreams also, it became my primary motivation to work even harder.

I was alone in a foreign land and thousands of miles away from home. Mind you, this was just the second time I was away from my family and it happened to be so far away. This time, I couldn't just hop on a bus and be home before supper. There were many times I felt so depressed, exhausted, lonely, and would think that I could not go on anymore. Not because of the four jobs I had: waiting tables from 5:30 to 8:30 in the morning; office clerk from 9 am to 5 pm; chambermaid from 6 pm to 11:30 pm; and cleaning 2 houses on weekends, but rather because I missed my loved ones so much that I would cry in my sleep almost every night. I remember asking, *"Why God, why me?"* But you know what? Sometimes, I really do impress myself with my ability to block my emotions so I can focus more on the important task that lies ahead. To this day, I still feel uneasy remembering those hardships. Don't get me wrong though. *I was very proud of those sacrifices and hardships because they allowed me to accomplish my goals!* I was tested beyond my limit, and having said that, I still can't for the life of me figure out how I overcame those *hardships!*

AGE: 25-31
FOLLOW YOUR HEART AND IDENTIFY YOUR PRIORITY!

After *four* long years of being away from my family, I finally was able to save enough to come back to the Philippines to visit them. And I also I married that wonderful, good looking guy I met at the town fiesta on April 6, 1977. His name is *Banny* and he later joined me in London, England in September 1979.

My life became easier with the passing of time and with my husband beside me, we were now able to do more to help several of my extended family who was in the Philippines. Unfortunately for us, we were not able to have children. I believe it was not meant to be.

AGE: 32-PRESENT
THE GOOD UNITED STATES OF AMERICA

We did not know at the time that there will be a far greater opportunity waiting for us in another place. My husband was accepted to work here in the USA as a Physical Therapist. He came to the USA in 1983, a couple of months ahead of me as we still had business to settle in London.

It seems like only yesterday when I remember the day I stepped foot in this country. It was like a new beginning for me. It was in early 1983 when I first arrived in Florence, South Carolina and had no idea what my life was going to be like in another strange land. But somehow, I knew in the back of my mind that it was going to be much better because America has the reputation for being the land of opportunity.

On *April 6, 2013*, we celebrated our *36th wedding anniversary*. In the middle of our celebration, we said, **"We're really proud of our marriage. It's the first for both of us, and the last!"**

- The Good Daughter from North Carolina (Accountant)

The Lioness Maiden (Division Manager of a Government Agency)

Since I was a young girl, it has been my dream to study at an exclusive school for girls, like Maryknoll, or St. Teresa's, or Holy Spirit. But considering our huge brood of 6 siblings, my parents had to manage and balance our limited earnings and resources. Moreover, exclusive schools were far from our home in Valenzuela, Bulacan resulting in higher tuition and transportation expenses. These make the fulfillment of my dream impossible and impractical. As a compromise, I landed at the University of the East-Caloocan High School (UECHS), the venue of my high school days — with cheaper tuition fees and much closer to home.

My mother was someone who would really plan and budget everything to ensure that the family is spending just enough, while still able to save some from my father's earnings. She always enrolled me early making it possible to be part of Section A, the most sought after section at UECHS.

AGE: 12-16

From 1st year to 4th year, I was in Section A resulting in the development of a close friendship among three (3) of classmates: Minaflor L (now Ms. S), Grace P (now Ms A), and Eden N (now Ms, B and deceased). We were so close to each other, as if we were sisters. We even composed a theme song for our group, which we called D' Glitters. Our theme song was to the tune of the famous Monkees' Song, "Hey, Hey we're the Monkees". We changed this title into "Hey, hey we're D' Glitters", and the song would run like this:

> "Hey, hey we're D' Glitters, kind and honest to all,
> We are always together, Yolly, Mina, Eden and Grace.
> If we will find you lonely, here are D' Glitters that will make you happy,"
> (Repeat)

Our group was happiest during our High School days. Our bonding even extended when we were in college. For Mina and I, we were still together even up to our work a GSIS (a government agency). We both worked in the same government corporation after graduating from college. Some of our weird and funny ways then were: bringing clothes to school and would change after class and pose for pictures in the different views of the school grounds. We would go together to Good Earth in Avenida to ensure that we can buy the same type, style of school shoes...; we would always go to different known eateries - any carinderia (specialty restaurants) that we heard was good and yummy. Our favorite past time was to eat at a famous carinderia in Tanong, Malabon: guinataan, halo-halo, bibingka, puto bumbong, pancit malabon, lugaw, tokwa't baboy and the unforgettable Nelia's halo-halo in Tinajeros, Malabon. We would even reach that place just to eat halo-halo and would you believe that I even brought my 1st and 2nd hubbies (unfortunately, both are now deceased. I've been widowed twice) there just to prove to them how delicious was the halo-halo, our barkada loved to eat during high school days. Then we would frequently visit Channel 9 where the famous 9 Teeners dance program was being aired, and at Channel 11 for the "Nite-Owl Dance Party" Eden and I even joined the dance contest. With humbleness perhaps I can share that I landed as a weekly finalist but didn't make it through to the monthly finals. Every after periodical exams, when dismissals were early, the four (4) of us would go to Manila, and watch movies, or go to Luneta Park; we also frequented the University canteen then, again to eat... These hobbies of ours, irked one of our teachers who often saw us there, eating, chatting, laughing...posing for pictures...

Despite our "barkada" thing, I believe that we were all also doing good in class, this was why I, and all of us (D' Glitters) wondered and were surprised what happened came graduation day. To our surprise we were not allowed to go to the graduation stage, and this has been the most frustrating and loneliest experience we had during high school...so disgusting!.. Frustrating!... Humiliating!... The hardest blow I had...we had....cause comparing ourselves to one classmates (safe not to mention name) of ours who was then was always the "kulelat" or lowest, last, in ranking every grading period...she was able to go up the stage...WOW!...and "us" why not?... As I was writing this portion of the narrative, my heart was pounding...I was hyperventilating... I HATE reminiscing this portion of my high school days...I hope that teacher realized what she did to us, to our life as senior students. Didn't she realize that it was supposed to be the happiest part of being high school, and we were denied that privilege? We were not "bobo" (stupid)... We were just happy high school students! And take note, our hobbies were just to eat and have fun... Studies were not being forgotten, and all of us promised and swore that we won't have boyfriends while in high school, and indeed we stayed with no boyfriends until after high school. As to my case, I had my first boyfriend when I was in 2nd year college at the University of the East, Manila.

Boys were not absent during high school days, but we kept our promise (blood compact with barkadas) not to have boyfriends or be committed while in school. It was so funny to reminisce though, my weird and funny experience with a suitor (need not mention, but I know so many knew about him/it especially from the boys department) and certainly, D' Glitters, all aware of it. This boy was so fond of singing "Light my Fire" whenever I passed the corridor, while he and his barkadas (group) were seated on the bench. I was so irritated then because he would even utter sensual words... So unbecoming of a gentleman. The most that I couldn't forget was when this boy together with his barkadas followed us when we went to the Malabon Public Library to conduct research to meet a school assignment. I was so scared because I still need to go home to Valenzuela unlike my friends who were all residing in Malabon. In my fear, I talked to the librarian who coincidentally lived in Maysilo, to accompany me in going home. She was so kind and understanding, she went with me in going home, hence, the boys in one car stopped following me. This boy even visited me in our house, and did still continued courting me until first year college, but really, my heart was not for him, hence, no matter how he tried, I said 'NO".

45

Unfortunately, my crush then had a girlfriend already, and I would smile once in a while every time I recalled when he played a guitar and sang the song "I Wanna Be Free" in our Biology class, while they were campaigning in the Student Council. I was imagining that he wanted to be free from his girlfriend and court me... This is just a thought.

AGE: 16-21

My college was a struggle to finish Business Administration majoring in Banking and Finance. A struggle, because most of the times, my parents are short of funds to finance my education. Just to finish, I would enroll only in a few units, sometimes 12 units every semester, and this was the reason why it took me five (5) years to finish college. But I can proudly say that I spared my parents from paying half of my tuition fees from the 2nd semester of 3rd year and the whole of 4th year because I got an automatic half scholarship grant from U.E for maintaining a final general average grade of 2. D' Glitters were still very active and alive then. We would usually meet, eat out (at Luisa & Sons or Little Quiapo or the famous Mamon Luk), go shopping, watch movies, etc. Then, getting together became less frequent when we were in our 2nd year college because each us had a boyfriend already by that time. Grace married early as well as Eden. Mina and I were left until we graduated and always together whenever applying for jobs. We ended up not being employed for a while. Then we decided to apply for a job separately.

AGE: 22-44

Considering that my father was with GSIS, he got me an appointment for entrance exam in the said office which I topped. I was employed as a casual general clerk for 3 years. While there, I continued convincing Mina to apply with GSIS too, which she did. She was employed there too. Happiness, fun continued, we were always together. Though we seldom see Grace and Eden, but we made sure the line of communication was maintained. Eden, who then put up her own dress shop, even made my wedding gown and that of the whole entourage in my 2nd marriage. Grace, after being widowed, was re married to an Iglesia ni Cristo Minister and settled for good in Baguio.

At the GSIS, I met my 1st husband, a Civil Engineer. We had 2 sons. I strived to be successful in my career to ensure a comfortable life and make my dream come true through my sons. Yes, that very dream, the dream of graduating from exclusive school for girls. I wanted to fulfill that dream through my sons.

When the Civil Service required a masteral degree to be promoted to a Division Chief at GSIS, I immediately applied for a scholarship grant. An exam was given, I passed it, and earned a scholarship. GSIS financed my masteral degree tuition fees with the condition that I maintain a grade of 2 until the final, or else I would have to reimburse all the tuition fees paid. I succeeded; I made it, maintained the required grade, and was then promoted to a Division Chief. I rose from the ranks until I retired in 2008 as Manager, after the then PGM Winston Garcia offered a very attractive Early Retirement Package. Almost 80% of qualified executives availed of it, including Mina and I.

When my 1st son was only 2, I already instilled in his mind that he would study in Ateneo de Manila (an exclusive school), such that whenever someone would ask him where he's going to study, he would immediately answer, "Ateneo de Manila". The same thing was inculcated to my 2nd son. I was really determined, despite high tuition fees to see my 1st and 2nd son enrolled in that prestigious school for boys. I really wanted fulfilling my dream through them. I prepared them for this. Such that at the age of 3 1/2, I already enrolled my 1st son, and when the time for my 2nd son came, he was in school already at that, same age, 3 and 1/2. My tears were uncontrollable when they both passed the entrance exam for Prep. I even got nervous at the experience I had for both sons because both of them left the examination room so early. I thought then, that they did not finish the exam. So tears of joy were really overflowing when I saw their names among those who passed the entrance in the Ateneo bulletin board. Their high school came and again they had to pass the entrance exam to verify if they are indeed deserving to continue their high school in Ateneo. Both of them passed again. My youngest passed the entrance again and graduated from the prestigious school Ateneo de Manila with a Masters Degree. My eldest son's choice was Civil Engineering which was not offered at Ateneo. He graduated at the University of Santo Tomas and passed the Board of Civil Engineering the following year. Then he took a masters in Transportation and Communication from the University of the Philippines (UP). My youngest pursued his a law course in U.P but stopped after 2 years when he was hired by Smart Communications.

I am proud to say that I am a fulfilled mother despite being widowed twice. Both of my sons completed their studies at exclusive schools.

AGE: 45-50

I was widowed the 1st time when my youngest was in Grade VII and my eldest was in 2nd yr college.

Life after the death of my 1st hubby became somewhat complicated because I met and married my former crush in high school. I had to balance my time between my sons and my 2nd hubby. Since my 2nd hubby didn't want to live in my own house, we had to rent a house close to my house where my sons lived. I would visit my sons every day before and after work to ensure that they were taken cared of and doing well. My second marriage was short-lived because a tragic vehicular accident took the life of my 2nd hubby. He passed on after 5 years of our being together.

Life should not stop due to tragedies. After the demise of my 2nd hubby, I occupied myself by joining the Rotary Club of Centennial Quezon City, becoming the Leader President of the club, and was appointed Deputy District Secretary of Rotary

International District 3780. After retirement, I am proud to say that I became active in our parish activities. I joined the Liturgy of the Hour group and provided support whenever there are religious activities/projects initiated by our parish priest.

AGE: 45-60

Despite the sad experience I had in High School, I cannot deny the fact that I still desired to really see some of my classmates/batchmates from UECHS. I made sure that I could attend the reunions. My first experience of attending reunion was the grand reunion held in 1999 at Pescadores, former Fishpond during our High School days. I attended said reunion together with Mina. Thank you to my batchmate, Doctor Gerry R for inviting us. Then this was followed by several 69ners mini reunions, one held in Malabon, at the place of a batchmate. The other one held at Fort Bonifacio where our batchmate Lt. Col Tony A was an active officer then. He suggested the place. Such reunion was fully attended, successful and with so much fun. Should I share that I even presented a Tango Dance in that reunion? Hahaha...I love it... My hobby, "dancing". Some former teachers were present there, too. But to frankly say, I did hope that the teacher responsible for us not being able to get to the stage during graduation was not around. We also held a mini reunion at our Go to Pares Restaurant at corner N. Domingo and P. Tuazon Streets, Cubao, Quezon City. At least 22 batchmates attended in that said reunion. Then the last reunion I attended in the Philippines was the one held at the Pool side of the 6th floor of my condominium. Again, such was a successful and happy reunion. I can say, it was somewhat a grandiose and special reunion, considering that batchmates from the US and Canada attended, and a total of 80 69ners were in attendance. Thanks to Oscar V, Jun H and Delia L for taking time to be on work leave to attend. We really appreciated their presence.

Because my retirement came unexpectedly, I decided to be a partner in a restaurant business (Goto Pares) in Quezon City, and also bought a condominium to be closer to the restaurant. The restaurant was successful in its 1st two years of operation, but we ultimately sold it after it started losing money.

Not being used to not working and considering I was still young, at least that was how I feet, I decided to try my luck in the US. My first visit in the US was in 2009. It was a business and pleasure trip. I brought back home several items to sell items such as perfumes, purses, bags, sunglasses, wrist watches, clothes. I got back the airfare spent and earned more out of the sales. The purpose of my 2nd visit to the US was business and pleasure too. I attended a 69ner's reunion which was held at Las Vegas. It was really a very happy and successful reunion too. Batchmates from Seattle (Susan A), from Toronto Canada (Jessie J), from New Jersey, (Oscar V), and from Vancouver, Canada (Delia L) took time out too and attended. Ooops, I should specially mention Boni R (now Mrs. P) who came from Philippines, just like me, likewise, to attend such reunion. I should share the excitement and joys experienced when we held a mini reunion in San Diego. I enjoyed the company of the newest attendee, Bernadette G, now Mrs. C. Followed by a joyous mini reunion at Valencia,

California, coinciding with Ed B's birthday. I was so glad to have met Lucy V, Virgie S, Sofia Y and Rey N. I should not forget the recently held reunion in Las Vegas. So glad to have seen new faces in the likes of Eufranda P (now Ms. Sagcal), Dra. Cristina M (Ms. A), and Venerando B. We were surprised again by the attendance of Delia L.

AGE: Over 60

During my 3rd visit, I decided to stay in the US. I will continue working while I am able to. Thanks to our batchmate David DLR and his wife Josie for accommodating and giving me a job. I owed to them my good fortune here.

To end, I can say, I learned to prove myself and became determined to succeed and reach my goal after that sad experience from high school.

LOOKING BACK

My words of advice for the next generation are numerous. Grab every opportunity that comes your way whether it be for personal or career development... There is a saying that opportunity knocks only once, hence, if there is ever a chance for advancement, go and grab it. Aim high. Treat all aspects of what you are doing as serious competition and, you should aspire to be a winner Be sure that you are not stepping on somebody else's foot in your quest to move forward. Always remember that there is "karma". What you do unto others will come back to you. Be fair to everyone around you. At the end of the day, ask yourself if you had been fair to everyone. Do not lie. This is the number one teaching that I imparted to my sons. Say sorry if you have did something wrong. Remember that God is not sleeping, He sees everything that you do. Manage your time. It is very important to have a schedule of your daily activities. If you are on time, you can always be sure that you will meet your commitments. Allot time for any unforeseen events. Lastly, always pray, ask for God's guidance and blessings in everything that you do...God should always be in the midst of all your activities.

- The Lioness Maiden (Division Manager of a Government Agency)

The Psychiatrist from California

I am a UE-Caloocan High School (UECHS) 1969 graduate. I am currently working as a full-time Psychiatrist for the Los Angeles County Department of Mental Health at the LA Sheriff's department/Women's Jail in Los Angeles, California for the past 9 years.

I was working in Cleveland Ohio for almost 15 years in the Psychiatric Emergency Room at Saint Vincent's Hospital.

I went to the UST College of Science and graduated in 1973. Then, I went to study medicine at UERM in Quezon City, and graduated in 1977. I spent a year of internship at the Veterans Hospital in Quezon City, and passed the medical board exam the same year.

I came to the U.S. in November 1978. It is still very vivid to me - it was Thanksgiving Day! Turkey was served during all my 3 plane connections – Manila to Guam; Guam to Honolulu; and, finally, Honolulu to San Francisco.

I was wearing brown boots and faux-fur coat, carrying a white guitar for one of my friends. The other passengers were looking at me, perhaps they thought I was Janis Joplin or Loretta Lynn! I was so excited when I saw San Francisco from the air; just like what I saw in various magazines and calendars. I said to myself, "I fulfilled my dreams/ambition that I wrote on the 1969 Panorama Alumni book – to be a doctor and go abroad." But that is just the beginning of a long struggle! The next step is to pass all the qualifying exams (I already passed 3) and board exams, to be able to go into residency training program, and a subsequent specialty training/fellowship.

For almost 6 months, I lived at the home of Angel and Nelly DLR, family friends, and older brother of David DLR – my classmate at UECHS and my first boyfriend. Our families remained friends even though we drifted ways. They are all very kind and good people.

I got married, but I was not so lucky, it ended after 5 years when my son, Dennis, was only 3 years old.

First, I had to find work to finance my review course. My parents were providing some financial assistance, but it was insufficient, so I decided to work as clerk at a Home Savings Bank. I did not tell my supervisor about my long term aspiration. I needed the money! I still laugh whenever I remember the first time I used the IBM Typewriter – I was wondering what that ball at the center of the typewriter was!

We moved to New York. I continued reviewing for the FLEX or Federal Licensing Exam while taking care of my son, Dennis – 3 years old at that time. He was very sweet and rambunctious. He has been the center of my life.

50

My marriage ended in 1984. [When I passed the ECFMG exam; my marriage ended]

I worked as cashier in Brentwood Long Island, New York – at a Carwash facility. I learned how to operate a cash register very well. I passed the FLEX with high scores. I was now looking for residency training programs, and received several interviews across the U.S. When I resigned from the car wash station, the other car wash personnel thought that I was moving to the newly opened Wall-Mart across the street. It was at this point that I informed them that I was physician by training.

With very limited funds and lots of hospital interviews to go to, I decided to buy a 2-month Grey Hound Bus Pass – hop on, hop off to various locations. I took the 2-1/2 year old Dennis to my aunt to Los Angeles, and he stayed there for 2 months while I was completing all my interviews across the country. My aunt really helped me a lot.

Since I only bought one Greyhound Bus Pass, I had to put Dennis on my lap whenever there is another paying passenger. And at night, he would be sleeping on my arms and lap. When he woke up and cried and screamed, the entire bus passengers would scream at me!

Dennis dropped one of his shoes in the bus toilet, so for the next 2 days of our 4-day journey to Los Angeles, he was only wearing 1 shoe. When my Aunt Tita Auring picked us up at the Greyhound Bus Station in Los Angeles, she could not stop laughing when she saw Dennis wearing only 1 shoe and smelling like vinegar.

After almost 2 months of hospital interviews all over the U.S., I picked up Dennis in Los Angeles, and took a bus heading back to New York.

One of my interviews was with the Tampa General Hospital in Tampa, Florida. Venerando Batas, a UECHS-69 batch mate, picked me up at the bus station and offered me to stay with him for a few days. At that time, Venerando already completed his medical/residency training. Through the years, Venerando and I kept in touch and later on, I would take my vacation at their house in Bay Shore, Florida.

I also met several of my medical school classmates again – either at the Review School, or during the exams, or when I was interviewing in various hospitals. Many of them passed, but others had yet to meet the requirements.

I was accepted for residency training in General Psychology in Cleveland, Ohio. The hardest decision I made was to send my son, Dennis, to the Philippines to live there for 3 years with my parents while I was completing my residency. The first year was extremely difficult. It was 1 year of internal medicine. We worked for 36 hours straight. I rented a duplex across the emergency room of the hospital so I didn't have to drive. This was also the first time I experienced winter for 8 months with snow up to 2-3 feet high around me. No classes during winter storm, but the hospital was always open so we had to work, there were no holidays, no vacation, no exceptions!

When I was on my third year of training, my schedule was less hectic and no night calls. It was at this point when I asked my mother to take back Dennis to Ohio; this was late in 1986. Fortunately, I was able to get a live-in baby sitter/helper (the mother of one of our hospital nurses). The baby sitter/helper loved to play bingo during weekends. So, when I had to go to the hospital to work, she would take Dennis to her Bingo place. So Dennis learned to play bingo at the age of 6!

I finished the 4 years of training in General Psychiatry, and completed a fellowship in Drug Abuse, Treatment and Rehabilitation at the Cleveland Clinic Foundation in 1989.

And the rest is history.

- The Psychiatrist from California

The Doctor from Tampa, Florida (Faculty at University of South Florida College of Medicine)

Graduating from a public elementary school, the natural transition is to enroll in a public high school. However, coming from Navotas, there was no public high school and my choices were Arellano High, or St James Academy in Malabon, or University of the East-Caloocan High School (UECHS). As St. James was quite expensive, my parents decided to enroll me at UECHS as my *older sister Dolly was already studying there.*

I entered high school with less anxiety as my childhood friend and second cousin also decided to go there. Victor Hugo and I grew up together in Navotas. We were always together since elementary. Victor was a superb pianist as his mom was a piano teacher. He also excelled in declamation contest- I remember his version of "O captain, my captain".

Height is might, is it really? Being one of the vertically challenged in class and being "baby faced", I was always bullied by the so called "jocks". I would automatically stand in the very front of the line, and inside the classroom would sit at the very front.

Academically, I felt I did not do badly. I was always elected secretary except in the 4th year due to my supposedly nice penmanship. I contacted chicken pox during my sophomore year and affected my performance in the classroom.

I vividly remember being actively involved in decorating our classroom during Christmas time. Hermie Chua particularly was the prime mover. He was very artistic. I remember him taking me to ABS-CBN television for an audition at Tawag ng Tanghalan. He sang "Unchained Melody"- he did not make it.

I remember also running as senator in the student council under the party of David Paraiso. If my memory serves me right, we won by a landslide. David was bribing students with fresh Ilang–Ilang flower from their trees at home. Remigio Burgos also comes to mind on school political issues. He would describe Paraiso's viewpoint as "you and your foolish imagination". How about Ofelia Diaz, our class valedictorian- her opening greeting during election campaign was " Good morning, yours truly is Ofelia Diaz..."

ROTC

Wow, the first thing that comes to mind is "white side wall" haircut. I never liked ROTC- I always dreaded Saturday morning...up early and put on the entire ROTC regalia, then drill, march under a sunny sky in a very hot day.

ROMANCE

Now here comes the boy-girl infatuation. I always found Bernadette as attractive not just physically but also intellectually. I asked her to be my partner during our graduation ball dinner. Honestly, I don't remember if she agreed but all I know was she was seated next to me at the dinner table at Fish Fun Restaurant in Letre, Malabon. I have not seen Bernadette since graduating from high school.

Lessons learned:

There were blood, sweat and tears indeed during my high school years. I learned how to overcome my shortcomings and used them as a driving force to enter college. I also realized that with tenacity and faith I could achieve more despite being vertically challenged. I also learned there were more to life outside the classroom. Trying to balance academics, extracurricular activities, and dealing with raging hormones were very stressful and challenging. Despite all these, I felt I was a winner.

UE MAIN: 16-20 YEARS OLD

Now, I decided to enroll to the mother campus. Initially, I wanted to major in chemistry but later changed my mind to pre-med. My 2 other sisters were in medical field (medical technology and nutrition) who encouraged me to eventually go to medical school.
It was indeed a cultural shock for me to enter a university with about 60,000 students (almost like a town). The place was a maze. Going up and down the stairs was elbow to elbow. Again my favorite spot in the classroom was the very front seat. Commuting from Navotas to UE Manila was quite daunting. My first class was always at 730AM. I also had one class at night (non available during the day) and that was

not fun as I had to commute twice during Tuesdays-Thursdays-Saturdays. However, I found it convenient to go to St Jude novena on Thursdays night after class. In one of those nights when I was coming home, I was robbed at knife point by 4 men in Divisoria - only thing they took was my new wrist watch given to me by my grand aunt. I was devastated and learned a lot from this experience.

I knew I will do well in undergraduate as my favorite subjects were sciences. I took the dreaded MCAT. I remember Gerry Ramos as we had common friend, Nila. I applied to 3 medical schools (UERM, UST and UP) and got accepted to all of them. Lesson learned: my persistence, hard work and faith prevailed; material things were replaceable but successes in classrooms were not. I felt fortunate to have been accepted to the 3 medical schools I applied. My major hurdle was conquered - I was able to prove that" I can do it".

UERM: 21-24 YEARS OLD

Circa June, 1973: Excerpt from the late UP College of Medicine Dean Florentino Herrera: "Welcome Class 1977, the cream dela cream, the only medical school across the Pasig River".

Wow, the competition was tight right off the bat. I was surrounded by multitalented students (many also were graduates of Philippine Science High School). In my subgroup of 5, 3 were summa cum laudes (1 from UP Diliman, 1 from St. Paul's College and 1 from Silliman U, and the other 1 is a cum laude from UP Diliman.) At that time, there were many pre meds from UP Diliman that did not make the cut off grade. There were many political activists and their grades suffered. There were a number of us from UE Manila that made it. We were all either cum , magna or summa cum laudes.

Medical schooling was not for the faint of heart. It required a lot of sacrifice across the board. I joined Phi Kappa Mu fraternity. Fraternity life was a good learning experience...there is life outside the classroom. It helped me developed my social skills, camaraderie, and most importantly spirit of brotherhood. This is a lifetime commitment and I have no regret. Even when I was in medical school my boyish looks continued. I was invited to a few senior high school prom and nursing school parties. St Paul College was right next door. Clinical clerkship was quite exhausting as you go on duty very frequently, depending on rotation up to 24 hours every other day. Finally, graduation was held at Abelardo Hall in UP Diliman. I remember how proud my mother was (unfortunately, my dad passed away a year prior from a cancer). One by one, Dean Herrera called our name to receive the diploma. "From

Navotas, Metro Manila, Dr. Venerando Ignacio Batas". Our yearbook described me as follows" Dr. Bata, New Yorker from Navotas, many hoped he will never grow old out of his cuddly harmlessness."

Internship at PGH also was very challenging. It was physically and intellectually demanding. As part of the training, we had to do rural work. I was assigned at Los Banos, Laguna. I thought I was lucky, as I was able to go home every weekend. I was fortunate enough to have a rich benefactor there whose house was inside UP Los Banos campus. Rural medicine introduced me to a different perspective of health care delivery.

Romance: I also dated a Paulinian nursing student for about 2 years. She was charming and taught me a lot on other things in life- movies, concerts, parties (swaray).
Lessons learned: "one is not enough, two is never too much", my philosophy during medical school...study, study, study. Hard work pays off. Also, there is more to life than medical schooling.

MIGRATION TO USA/ LIFE IN THE LONE STAR STATE OF TEXAS: 27-30 YEARS OLD

Before migrating to US in 1980, I held a small clinic in Navotas for about 6 months. I was on my own. Nobody was teaching me on what to do. I did house calls. I did suturing of minor lacerations. I learned to be more independent and my level of maturity rose fast.

I joined my family (mother and sister) in Houston, Texas in March, 1980. I applied to different residency programs. I was lucky to get into a prestigious program, Baylor College of Medicine, Physical Medicine and Rehab. First time in my life, I was able to earn some money. I bought my first car and rented my own apartment. Being a foreign medical graduate wasn't easy as you have to prove yourself to everybody. I read a lot, researched a lot and published. I developed leadership skills and by the senior year, I was the chief resident. I passed all my boards and by the end of my residency training, I was all set to engage in full private practice.

1983-PRESENT; 30-60 YEARS OLD

Welcome to Sunshine State, Florida. I was recruited by a group of doctors in Tampa. At first, I was an employee for 2 years then became a full partner on my third year. My senior partners have retired and I became the president and CEO in 2008. I continued to challenge myself and in 1993 accepted an appointment as Medical Director of Tampa General Rehabilitation Center. To this date, II continue to serve as medical director and chief of Physical Medicine and Rehabilitation department.

In my early years in Tampa, personally something was lacking. I was finally introduced by a friend to his distant relative by the name of Lizza Jimenez. Lizza (was living in Manila)and I were basically pen-pals. Lizza graduated from UP, School of Economics, 1984. She finally immigrated to Los Angeles in 1985 where I personally met her for the first time. Needless to say I was attracted to her. We finally said "I do" in 1987. We are now blessed with 3 boys, Brian (25), Brent (22) and Bradley (14). Brian is a 4th year medical student at University of South Florida, Brent just graduated with a degree in Electrical Engineering and Computer Science from UC Berkeley and is now involved in setting up a startup company with his classmate. Bradley is a freshman in high school. I am proud to say that my boys were all chess champs. They competed nationally in the USA. All of us including Lizza, are tennis aficionados. We play regularly and compete as much as we can. We regularly travel around the world and enjoy skiing, snorkeling, hiking, fishing, whitewater rafting and rapelling. I couldn't ask for more and I thank God for being kind to us.

Professionally, I continue to work full time and teach medical students and residents. I currently hold a faculty position at University of South Florida College of Medicine. I am also busy travelling round the USA accrediting Rehabilitation Centers.

SUMMATION

Coming from a family that was not financially well off and the bullying I experienced in high school gave me strong motivation to excel in other aspects of life. I was neither athletic nor a movie star potential so the only way to go was to excel academically. Medical schooling at UP was not for the faint hearted. Everyone was brilliant and competition was stiff. In the end, it worked well as I feel I developed to a more mature and responsible individual. As a foreigner in USA, I realized that the only way to gain respect was to prove yourself as a productive and invaluable member of society. Never waver on what you believe is right.

Dealing with personal and professional life continues to be a balancing act. Parenting is a unique experience that cannot be bought or planned. If I have to do it all over again, I wouldn't change the path I travelled.

I would like to close by saying this verse from the Bible: Corinthians 13:13 which best describe my philosophy in life....

"FAITH, HOPE AND LOVE, THE GREATEST OF THESE IS LOVE."

- The Doctor from Tampa, Florida (Faculty at University of South Florida College of Medicine)

The Doctor from Caloocan

My high school years (1st to 4th) were a rich combination of anxieties, challenges, competition, conflict, doubt, expectation and excitement. You always think of what will be the next day's class activities; you become faced with assignments that challenge your mental capacities, your natural instinct to outsmart your classmates or even excel in some respects, expect a higher grade compared to previous grading period, you sometimes get involved in verbal or physical conflicts over some sensitive and vital classroom issues in particular or school in general; you doubt your teachers' being fair and just to all his/her students, and excitement for attaining a certain goal, academically speaking. Just to cite some instances: You could always tell a student who was facing Miss Francisca Agcaoili's famous physics: eyes wide with terror, a tendency to reply to "hello" with a dissertation on the Second Law of Thermodynamics. But, hard as we had to hit the books, we always got the support we needed: from the faculty and, even more importantly, from each other. I'll never forget spending the night with Ely Mendoza and Ricardo Rosali and Romy Ompoc (being the director) as we practiced the dramatization of the life of Diego Silang from our book Diwang Ginto for our Pilipino III subject under Mrs. Visitacion Adelino. This was typical. At UE, we worked together as we were all aware that the program in this institution was an academically demanding one. Of course also played together, we reserved a portion of time to relax by gallivanting around the campus, sauntering along the corridors of the Academic and Administration buildings and taking some glimpse of some winsome third year coeds, as well as some notable batchmates.

Now we got into college. Prior to this, I was really caught in a dilemma, or total indecision as what course to take up. I had three courses in mind: 1. JOURNALISM (I was challenged by Mr. Bayona) 2. FINE ARTS (I am a God-gifted artist, but my rationale: why should I enroll into a course that's already innate in me?)   and   3. MEDICINE (which to me was a disillusion, since my father's wherewithal was not commensurate with the cost and expenses in a medical course. Luckily, it was co-incident that 3 of my siblings migrated and worked abroad. They financed my medical studies from the start to finish.

Having had finally made up my mind, I enrolled at U.E. Manila as a Pre-Med student, leading to the degree of Bachelor of Science

U.E (Main) was totally a different campus and environment at that, what with an overwhelming population of over 68,000 (as Vernie had earlier mentioned). Academic situation was tough and too demanding, but this these gave me the inspiration and challenge to exert more effort because I had earlier on realized that the higher the general weighted average you obtain, the better the chance to enter the Medicine proper, particularly the highly acclaimed medical colleges like the U.P.

59

and U.E.R.M.M.C. (I obtained only 2.50,which was not competitively adequate enough). Among our batchmates in UECHS who became my classmates in some science subjects were VERNIE BATAS (in Zoology 6 or Comparative Embryology and Chemistry 10 of Physical Chemistry) and my platoon mate in R.O.T.C. (although he was assigned as First Aider) and VIRGIE SUMABAT (yes, she ambitioned to be a doctor too, as she had put it in the PANORAMA). By the way, our common friend was MARY NILA CAMELLO. Now here comes the period of applying for medical proper, the hassles and bustles associated with it. To pass the MCAT (Medical College Admission Test), you've got to score at least 90 out of a total items of 240 (I got 110). Another qualifying examination was to contend and hurdle the examinations given by a medical school (I only applied enrolled at MCU which was a walking distance from my place of residence). Luckily, I placed number 75 in a quota of 200 medical students admitted, from out of a thousand examinees.

LIFE AT MANILA CENTRAL UNIVERSITY

Being a medical student is a completely and totally different phase of one's life as a career student. The program and curriculum are, compared to Pre-Medicine, even more overwhelmingly tough, demanding, challenging, mentally exhausting, physically taxing, intimidating or daunting to say the least. As what Mark Anthony had stated (at Julius Caezar's funeral): "Ambition is made of sterner stuff!". Mediocrity, procrastination and devil-may-care attitudes have no place in the college; either you shape up or you ship out, it's your choice; it's your life anyway. I was surrounded by no-non sense medical students, matter of fact a handful of them came from UP (as Pre-Med). My first year was not quite burdensome, actually I even came to experience my name being placed in the bulletin board cabinet as an award of acknowledgment for those who have excelled in one particular departmental examination. But then as I stepped up to higher levels, I found the course getting increasingly formidable; but I promised myself not to quit, and it's not in my system nor in my personality. (Only the coward does).

THE BREAKDOWN

Third year medical proper is admittedly a known fact to be the "waterloo" for all medical students; it is the measuring gauge of your mettle, of your intelligence quotient.

Typically, this is the year with the most number of subjects which in effect, overwhelm, drown and mentally drain a medical student. And this was the predicament I got subjected into. Simultaneously, I got enamored with a certain classmate, but what I thought to be an inspiration turned out to be a desperation...I was spurned. I was totally devastated, and this spelled the doom on me, it adversely affected my studies, to the point of neglecting and eventually flunking a minor semestral subject; I had to repeat it for another semester, and not being allowed to get promoted to the fourth year level (clerkship or clinical experience). Lesson learned: Love is not always an inspiration for it may adversely affect your education resulting from desperation. Eventually, I graduated in 1978 (supposed to be 1977), where I placed number 54 from a graduating class of 120. Then we were required to take the REVALIDA (a qualifying exam for internship). There were ten of us candidates (along with other nine graduates who had the same case or predicament like mine as I have divulged above). I topped the exam with a score of 84; one was unsuccessful, and she had to take the ORAL REVALIDA as one last chance or remedial exam to qualify for the internship.

I had my post-graduate one year rotating internship at the FAMILY CLINIC HOSPITAL (1978 - 1979) and took and passed the PHYSICIAN'S LICENSURE EXAMINATION given in December of 1979.

Soon after registering at PRC and getting my license, I applied at MCU for a residency training in surgery, but while waiting for approval, I ventured to work at the Family Clinic Hospital as a resident physician just to occupy myself and while away the time. Until I got too much involved professionally and socially at the FCH such that my interest for training at MCU got shelved. So I just managed to concentrate and make good in my training in Family Medicine at FCH, where I graduated in December 1985).

AGE: 33-60 (LIFE AS A PRIVATE MEDICAL PRACTITIONER)

Life outside hospital practice is a totally different dimension and horizon in my medical career. The first two years are quite asthenic so to speak. It took several more years before I got established. I'm still active till the present.

DEVELOPMENTS ASSOCIATED IN MY PERSONAL LIFE

Just to sort of back track, I came to get acquainted with a staff nurse at the FCH (Family Clinic Hospital) which blossomed into a blissful relationship, that eventually led into marriage when I was almost... 41! Unfortunately, we were not blessed with a child.   The year 1997 was my turning point in my life. That was exactly 20 years after my immigrant petition (by my brother) got approved. So along with my wife, we left the Philippines and migrated to Hawaii on May 24, 1997. Not too long thereafter, I found out that Virgie Sumabat was already residing in Santa Clara, California who was then working as a certified nursing attendant. She invited us couple over to move to her place and join her with her late dad. I was to and fro the Philippines and California the next two years (every 6 months just to protect my green card) since I really could not relinquish or give up my medical practice. But this setting on my part, eventually led me to realize it was boring, cumbersome, physically taxing, and most of all, quite expensive, not to mention the negative effect to my practice.

LONG DISTANCE RELATIONSHIP

Ignoring all odds and the intuitions from acquaintances and my siblings, I opted to maintain a long distance relationship with my wife. But fate had it that this arrangement would really yield negative results. Something went wrong and we drifted apart....for good!

Having had managed to move on, I came to realize I had to put more focus more and intensify the level of zest in my professional practice; such that the only other two things that occupy my time till the present time are: 1) to attend to the activities of the Philippine Medical Association and the Caloocan City Medical Society where I am currently the vice-president, and 2) to attend occasional separate get-together gatherings with my high school batch mates and with my section mates as well as general alumni homecomings of the U.E. (batches 1957 to 1982).

So on the side, occasionally, I would reminisce everything of the above trivia and milestones in my life; and if I only have my way to turn back the hands of time, and become once again a youthful 13 year-old greenhorn high school student, I would reformat, redesign, or 'turn over a new leaf' so to speak, my style and strategies in my ways of studying and learning as well as develop my competitive instinct and eliminate my inferiority complex and aloofness to become a sociable individual.

As a legacy for the present generations (which actually belong to the two or three more generations after me, or us) allow me first to mention two favorite adages in my recollection: "Time is gold and that, procrastination is the greatest thief of time" and "There is a knowledge which cannot be written down but can only be passed down by example; let not the excellence in your training (professional or technical) blind you to what you lack in other respects."

Continue to strive; continue to achieve. Gather strength as you gain more laurels. Our changing society demands more strength, greater impetus in the pursuit of ideals. We are presently revolving in a fast-changing world where only the agile, the involved, the resourceful. so it seems, can truly survive. In your involvement, soon you will find yourselves confronted with deeper and more vital issues - political, social, or economic where your own integrity, your sincerity, and your power of endurance or stamina will be put to a grueling test. When this crucial time comes, and surely it will come, your Alma Mater will be keeping guard, confident of your success for she has fully equipped you with tools essential for achievement, for distinction, and with an exuberant feeling of pride that she is a part of the personal honor and glory which you will have earned. Go forth young men and best wishes! With this, I conclude my narrative, I bid you goodbye!

Thank you.

- The Doctor from Caloocan

The Dreamer (Accountant and USAF Reserve from California)

I am a jack of all trades and master of none, no profession and no skills, just somebody who wants to survive, to make living in the US worthwhile.

I came to the University of the East-Caloocan High School (UECHS) on my third year in high school, and this is the third high school I attended. I like UECHS so much, I didn't have to look for a fourth one. Back then, I thought it was the worst thing to happen to transfer schools, but now I realized I have the pleasure to attend three high school reunions and meet old friends.

Although, UECHS provided a lot of experiences and knowledge to prepare me for college, it's my elementary school that I gave credit for building my foundation spiritually and academically. This is where I became aware of children of rich and famous of Malabon and Navotas, being driven to school, that I dream of becoming financially independent and retire early. I remember when I was in the 5th grade, I already know how to make promissory note and forged my father's signature. I spent 3 months tuition fee on pinball machines, and I cannot take the final exam without paying it. The school let me take the exams with my promissory note and I thought, I got the problem solved. Until registration came for the following year, I cannot register without the report card. I told my father that I lost the report card, even my father helped looking for the report card that I never got. My father and I went back to the school, and he found out that my report card is in the school, and was on hold because of the unpaid tuition. On the way home, we're both silent. Perhaps, he was thinking what kind of punishment he's going to give me, and I was thinking of the same thing. I got it alright, but did not get it right away. He told me to lie down on the floor and I waited almost the whole afternoon. It was an agonizing wait, every time I hear footsteps, I thought, here it comes. Hours passed, and I thought, maybe I won't get it after all. Well, wrong again, he was just waiting for the right timing.

High school life could be describe as mostly academics, joining student organizations, looking at girls/boys and flirting with each other. This is also the time that is most enjoyable and memorable for me. That's when I started hanging out with friends, attend parties, play records and just listen to favorite songs. Hard to admit, I learned how to drink beer and smoke. One group which I'm proud to be a member is the Boy Scouts, not because I'm the scoutmaster, but rather I learned leadership, to be responsible, self-discipline, different skills and enjoyed the camaraderie. Camping to remote places with only basic necessities taught me how to be independent. Being responsible to UECHS administration and parents, I made sure our activities were safe and nobody misbehaved.

The one organization that stood out of during this period was the Boy Scouts Troop of UECHS and its adviser Mr. Buenavista, and the past leaders of Troop #10. Our group's activities was confined not only to the campus of UECHS but also extended outside the campus. It's like a fraternity, in which our friendship extends beyond our high school life but into our family life.

YEARS: 1969-73

College came and I went to UST Engineering for 2 years and changed course, moved to UE Main to get my Degree in Business Administration majoring in Accounting and minor in Economics. Right after taking my CPA exam, I worked briefly at Philippine Banking Corporation as bookkeeper in the Foreign Department. I left for the United States in June 1975, in high hopes that I will finally fulfill my dream to be financially independent. When I got to America I found out that it was not easy. I went thru the challenges, struggles, and hardships of being an immigrant in America. I found a job right away but the salary is not what I thought that will make me rich and retire at the age of 45. After taxes, my salary is just enough for my expenses, whatever was left went to the car and its expenses. So, I thought about getting a second job, and that's how I ended up working for the USAF Reserves. After I read a brochure for the military, I was very impressed that I joined right away, thinking that I can be a flight engineer. I found out after Basic Training in Texas, that I need to wait to be a Sergeant, to be considered in the program. I qualified after a year, but did not pursue, I do not want to do the jungle survival training. I stayed in the Reserves for six years and one of the positive things I got from it, is my wife. I met her at USAF Technical School in Illinois, who happened to live in the same city and went to the same reserve unit at Travis Air Force Base, California. We got married in 1977, two months after I started working for Stanford University. We have a son and a daughter.

YEARS: 1977-2001

I worked at the comptroller's Office for a year and transferred to Stanford Linear Accelerator Center, working for another twenty-four years until I retired at the age of 51 years old. I went thru apprenticeship training for four years and attended school for two years after work. Acquiring my journeyman level, I worked as a Lab Mechanician working on prototypes use for research for the U. S. Department of Energy. With a baby on the way, I was determined to buy a house. So, I got a second job, working at the U.S. Postal Service, while still going to school and doing my air force job, one weekend a month.

YEARS: 2001-PRESENT

As we enter the twilight of our life, we looked back and ponder, how did we do in our life. Each one of us, have our goal, some are loftier than the other and for some a simple one just to finish high school, have a good job and a family. Most will think of our accomplishment, success, wealth we accumulated, how high we reached the job ladder, or whatever our status is, all of this is worthless upon our death. Rather, there's a question that we will be asked, and that's how successful we are in following God's will.

To my family, relatives, friends and batchmates, (like the song "Bridge Over Troubled Waters"), in your worry, in your struggles, I'm with you and in your triumph, I'm behind watching you.

BRIDGE OVER TROUBLED WATER – SIMON AND GARFUNKLE

http://www.youtube.com/watch?v=UVDg8fVC4EQ

When you're weary, feeling small
When tears are in your eyes
I will dry them all

I'm on your side
Oh when times get rough
And friends just can't be found

Like a bridge over troubled water
I will lay me down
Like a bridge over troubled water
I will lay me down

When you're down and out
When you're on the street
When evening falls so hard, I will comfort you

I'll take your part
Oh, when darkness comes
And pain is all around

Like a bridge over troubled water
I will ease your mind
Like a bridge over troubled water
I will ease your mind

Sail on silver girl, sail on by
Your time has come to shine
All your dreams are on their way
See how they shine

Oh, if you need a friend
I'm sailing right behind

Like a bridge over troubled water
I will ease your mind
Like a bridge over troubled water
I will ease your mind

(continued...)

I promised my wife that before I die, I'll write my autobiography that they can read on my memorial service, thanks to David Paraiso's effort, you don't have to wait for that moment.

LOOKING BACK

Like my advice to my children, put God first in all of our actions, be serious in their education and avoid bad company. Life is like driving a car, we are the driver, and we got control of the car (life). We can choose to be a good or bad driver. There are many ways to reach our destination, straight, winding or dirt road. There might be potholes and detours along the way, and it's up to us to overcome it. There are rules or laws to follow and if we choose to disregard the rules and get caught, we should be prepared to suffer the consequences, and pay the penalty. Like a good driver, if we obey all the rules, then it will be a smooth trip to afterlife.

My life, when I was 14-16 yrs old, was one of the most enjoyable and rewarding part of my life and I don't have any regret about it. It's not outstanding but it's not bad either. If I had a second chance to be that age again, I will not change any part of it, not one bit.

-   The Dreamer (Accountant and USAF Reserve from California)

The Mentor from California

CLOSING REMARKS AT THE UECHS REUNION on 6/22/2013 in Las Vegas, Nevada
<portions of this were shared with the participants during the event>

For our batch today - we are hovering around 60-61 years old, give and take a couple of months; compared to when we were collectively together as 14-16 olds in 1969 - 44 years ago.

My objectives are primarily to share insight and experience that might resonate to some of us – then and now - and, hopefully trigger productive endeavors down the line. One of those endeavors, within 1 year, is to collect and publish a collective experience of growing up from volunteers. In so doing, I will be back-tracking and fast-forwarding between 1969 thru today, an elapsed period of 44 years.

- I thank, Julie Bolda, Cristy Mendoza, David de Los Reyes and others who made this and supporting events possible.
- Special thanks and appreciation to Cristy Mendoza who provided support and venues of 3 adjacent units at the Marriott's Grand Chateau, Las Vegas-NV and subsequent events.
- The messages of this speech are intended for the UECHS batch of 1969, their spouses, family friends, guests, the world, and anybody who cares to take the time and listen.
- Let us honor and remember those who have departed and who have been a part of what we are today, and what the next generations will be, our mentors: Director Abanilla, Assistant Director Santiago, Mrs. Abaya, Mr. Mirasol, Mr. Bayona, Mrs. Gamalinda, other members of the 1969 faculty and supporting school staff, our classmates, and many others. As individuals, we were molded by these role models, events, dreams, aspirations, hopes, and tragedies.
- Let us be mindful and sensitive that after 1969, the batch of UECHS could be categorized into at least 3 groups: (1) those who immigrated to other countries, (2) those who were Overseas Contract workers, and (3) those who remained in the homeland. The fortunes, options and destinies of each of us are directly proportional to which group one belongs to.
- Almost every major event in my life, I can fondly associate with the UECHS experience; the experience has a special a place in my heart, which transformed me to what I am today. For reasons I could neither understand nor explain, that period of my life is much more endearing and lasting than the years prior, and the years after. It is probably due to the unique fusion of various cultures, the camaraderie, innocence, idealism, energy, hope, aspirations, tragedies, cynicism - which can never be duplicated at different times.
- 44 Years ago – we were 15-16 years old. That means that there were 44

batches which came after us, and perhaps at least 10 batches that preceded our batch.

- Life could be viewed as consisted of 3 stages. Assuming that one's life span is at least 60 years – the first 1/3 (1-20 years old) – is when we grow up and educate ourselves; the second 1/3 (21-40 years old) – when we build a career and raise a family; the last 1/3 (41-and beyond) – is when we do whatever we really want to do, like being grandparents, volunteering for noble cause, and others.

This said, let me shift gear and reinforce one of my messages by sharing the plot of a movie "About Schmidt" – starring Jack Nicolson in 2002 (http://en.wikipedia.org/wiki/About_Schmidt).

Warren Schmidt (Jack Nicolson) is retiring from his position as an actuary with Woodmen of the World, an insurance company in Omaha, Nebraska. Schmidt is given a retirement dinner that seems to bring no comfort. Schmidt finds it hard to adjust to his new life outside of work, feeling useless. One evening, he sees a television advertisement about a foster program for African children, Plan USA, and decides to sponsor a child. He soon receives an information package with a photo of his foster child, a small Tanzanian boy named Ndugu Umbo, to whom he relates his life in a series of candid, rambling letters.

Before leaving Denver, Schmidt composes a letter to Ndugu. Schmidt questions what he has accomplished in life, lamenting that he will soon be dead, that his life has made no difference to anyone, and that eventually it will be as if he has never existed at all.

A pile of mail is waiting for him at home. Schmidt opens a letter from Tanzania. It is from a nun, who writes that Ndugu is illiterate but appreciates Schmidt's letters and financial support very much. A painting drawn by Ndugu is enclosed, showing two smiling stick figures, one large and one small, holding hands on a sunny day. The film ends with Schmidt weeping as he looks at it.

In the autumn of our lives, how many of us associate ourselves with Schmidt in this movie?

- During those times, there were five major influences, among many, which laid the foundation for what I would become. (1) My parents surrounding us-children with educational materials – Life Magazines and Science series, National Geographic, History, Engineering, Smithsonian, Encyclopedia and others. To this day, my interest on learning is vigorously pursued via npr.org, pbs.org, c-span.org, history.com, smithsonianchannel.com and others. (2) Uncle Benjamin, the eldest brother of my mother and a physician, who inculcated and nurtured the value of learning, and encouraged me to access his extensive library focusing on the sciences and philosophy. Uncle Benjamin's tutelage is best illustrated in the movie - Gran Torino (http://en.wikipedia.org/wiki/Gran_Torino) where Walt Kowalski (Clint Eastwood) was showing the tools in his garage to his protégé' Thao Vang Lor (Bee Vang). In the film, Walt Kowalski was a recently widowed Korean War veteran alienated from his family and angry at the world. Part of my message in this narrative is in the "Gran Torino" with Clint Eastwood and "About Schmidt" with Jack Nicolson. (3) The progressive and social activism role of the United Methodist church (please note that former Secretary of State Hillary Clinton is an ardent Methodist). (4) A strong-willed mother who provided unqualified support and resources often at the expense of her own comfort. Collectively, these provided me with models and mentors from various communities, cultures, generations and millennia around the world, which were well beyond what were available and accessible within our own immediate community and borders. (5) My grandfather- Pio, and my father who have been always there for me.

- I transferred as a Junior to UECHS in 1966. I was an innocent boy of 14. I originated from a sheltered and overprotected family in Malabon, Rizal. When I graduated from UECHS still as a boy of 16 in 1969, I was transformed to a part dreamer, part cynic, part fighter, part builder, part saint, part monster, and part who knows what else? Clearly, the 2 years at UECHS accelerated my maturity and transformation - for better and worse. Just like everybody, through these and following years, I had to manage my demons.

As early as that age of 14 and hopefully until I fade away, my approach to life is best described by a quote from the MAN IN THE ARENA, an excerpt from the speech "Citizenship In A Republic" delivered by President Theodore Roosevelt at the Sorbonne, in Paris, France on 23 April, 1910:

"It is not the critic who counts; not the man who points out how the strong man stumbles, or where the doer of deeds could have done them better. The credit belongs to the man who is actually in the arena, whose face is marred by dust and sweat and blood; who strives valiantly; who errs, who comes short again and again, because there is no effort without error and shortcoming; but who does actually strive to do the deeds; who knows great enthusiasms, the great devotions; who spends himself in a worthy cause; who at the best knows in the end the triumph of high achievement, and who at the worst, if he fails, at least fails while daring greatly, so that his place shall never be with those cold and timid souls who neither know victory nor defeat."

- My sheltered and overprotected family, particularly my grandfather and father reminded me of the following:

From Psalms 23

69

The LORD is my shepherd; I shall not want.
He maketh me to lie down in green pastures:
 he leadeth me beside the still waters.
He restoreth my soul:
 he leadeth me in the paths of righteousness for his name's sake.
Yea, though I walk through the valley of the shadow of death,
 I will fear no evil: for thou art with me;
thy rod and thy staff they comfort me.
Thou preparest a table before me in the presence of mine enemies:
 thou anointest my head with oil;
my cup runneth over.
Surely goodness and mercy shall follow me all the days of my life:
 and I will dwell in the house of the LORD forever.

 - Author: The Bible

From Ecclesiastes 3

To every thing there is a season, and a time to every purpose under the heaven:
A time to be born, and a time to die; a time to plant, and a time to pluck up that which is planted;
A time to kill, and a time to heal; a time to break down, and a time to build up;
A time to weep, and a time to laugh; a time to mourn, and a time to dance;
A time to cast away stones, and a time to gather stones together; a time to embrace, and a time to refrain from embracing;
A time to get, and a time to lose; a time to keep, and a time to cast away;
A time to rend, and a time to sew; a time to keep silence, and a time to speak;
A time to love, and a time to hate; a time of war, and a time of peace.

 - Author: The Bible

- During those years and thereafter, I learned that the choices we make, what we say do and say, a word of kindness, and a sprinkle of understanding - could make the world a better, or worse place to live in. Like it or not, we become role models for others to emulate, or avoid. These might not necessarily save or alter the course of a nation, but those choices, deeds and words could mean all the difference and influence in the path and destiny of a family, a wife, a husband, a son or daughter, a grandson or daughter, a friend, our peers, a loved one, an associate, or even a casual observer, etc. So if you have something worthwhile to do and say, perhaps this is the time to do it...; because there will be no better opportunity to do or say it.

- One of the places which I find special, humbling and in being transformative is the airport. Even now, as I log in thousands of travel miles per week, every time I pass by or think of an airport, there is a part of me that wakes up in awe and wonders what's next?. For me, it is a place where the past, present and future meet; it is a place where the known meets the unknown. The airport is a portal, in each visit, it could be any combination of: the beginning, or continuation, or the end of a relationship. It is a venue for getting together after years of separation; or, permanent separation after years of alienation (like in the movies: War of the Roses with Michael Douglas and Kathleen Turner). As immigrants or Overseas Contract Workers, this is very personal. The same could be said of a train or bus station.
- Be careful what you say and do, there will be intended and unintended consequences among and across family members, peers, communities and generations.
- We create our own bubble - some lasts more than others, some are more illusion, some are a lot closer to reality.
- Other than the family and the church, most of the things that I do and say today, originated during those formative and fragile years at UECHS.
- There are times when I close my eyes, and I vividly remember those days: working at and chairing meetings at the Vision High School newspaper, the Panorama Alumni Book, and the Student Government; playing basketball, marching during the PMT/drill days on Saturdays; debating until late evenings; interacting with the UEC and UE Main College leadership; locking horns with the student leaders of various schools; strolling along the dusty Samson Road towards Sangadaan with the Los Palikeros to eat our mami and halo-halo, etc. For me these are voyages of discovery, exploration and serendipity of our peers and the world around us.
- Let us talk about fitting in or being accepted. Unlike most of you who spent most of the 4 years at UECHS during those high school years, where you had the opportunity to develop and nurture lasting bonds, I was a transfer from a rival school generally perceived as below UECHS in terms of status and achievements. As I recall it, the school faculty, organizations and groups did not welcome and made things very difficult for me before, during and after being elected and designated as the chair of the Student Government, Vision (the school paper) and Panorama (the alumni year book). Most of you did not know at that time, there was a time when my mother hired a security detail to protect me from bullying and harassments. Before the security detail, it was Leonardo Mendoza and R. Laboy who were my protectors and supporters. My mother also hired tutors who mentored me in the art of debates and organization. I say this now to highlight the strong and endearing bond between a mother and a son, and how a mother achieved her aspirations through a son. More significantly, imagine how this played out in the mind of a 14-16 old "transferee", and how this transformed a part of me which fights and makes things happen. Briefly, I persevered

and moved on.

- Let us talk about the crushes and loves of my life during and after those times. Briefly, because I represented the entire school internally, and externally where I worked with the leaderships of various schools – exclusive, non-exclusive and everything else in between included - I had numerous crushes and loves, except that none of them loved me. They probably did not even notice me. In short, the ones I liked could care less about me, and the ones who liked me, I did not notice either. Several among our batch, including me, developed relationships with disastrous consequences which I will rather not discuss in this forum.
- Let us talk about failures and sorrows. I have a lot of these, and as we speak, there are more coming this way. This will take a lifetime of narration and I do not want to ruin your evening listening to my pontification. I defer you to the MAN IN THE ARENA speech of Theodore Roosevelt which I narrated earlier. Using a methapor that best describe my character, I associate with Humphrey Bogart, Burt Lancaster and Toshiro Mifune in terms of being romantic, idealistic, cynical and practical, not necessarily at the same time. My favorite Director is Akira Kurosawa. For specifics, please refer to: Casa Blanca (http://en.wikipedia.org/wiki/Casablanca_(film) , We're No Angels (http://en.wikipedia.org/wiki/We%27re_No_Angels_(1955_film), Tough Guys (http://en.wikipedia.org/wiki/Tough_Guys_(1986_film), From Here to Eternity (http://en.wikipedia.org/wiki/From_Here_to_Eternity) , Valdez Is Coming (http://en.wikipedia.org/wiki/Valdez_Is_Coming), Akira Kurosawa (http://www.theguardian.com/film/filmblog/2010/mar/23/akira-kurosawa-100-google-doodle-anniversary, http://www.pbs.org/wnet/gperf/shows/kurosawa/kurosawa.html), Seven Samurais (http://en.wikipedia.org/wiki/Seven_Samurai), Toshiro Mifune (http://en.wikipedia.org/wiki/Toshiro_Mifune).
- One television series that resonate to me is the "Highway to Heaven" with Michael Landon and Jonathan Smith (http://en.wikipedia.org/wiki/Highway_to_Heaven) where Michael was an angel on probation and he helps various troubled souls to overcome their problems.
- Those formative years at UECHS taught me man's extraordinary gift, potential and capacity for transformation, compassion, to do good to others without being asked to do so, and without anything in return, as well as to cause destruction and harm of unbelievable brutality and magnitude to others and the world around us. Without mentioning names, there are those of us who have been doing these through the years.
- Leaving UECHS, is like losing the love of your life, except that at that time, I did not realize that the bonding and camaraderie will far outlive most of what I come to love and cherish; and as is the case with great relationships, we do not realize its endearing value and what it meant, until we lose it. And no matter how hard we try to recreate those days, it will not be the same.
- At UECHS the following were learned and reinforced: (1) Respect and honor

our creator, elders, the family and others; (2) the need for identifying and working with the best mentors and models who will guide and inspire me through the peaks and valleys, and the feast and famine of life– cradle through grave; (3) Being considerate of others and the disciple of restraining conceit; (4) The need to constantly reinvent and transform myself; (5) The need to be humble, to listen, and learn from others regardless of their status; (6) Staying healthy – physically, mentally, emotionally, etc.; (7) Knowing my limitations, as well as those people around me; (8) The need to persevere and to fight for causes worth fighting for, and to give up causes not worth my salt; (9) The need to develop my gifts and blessings, and in sharing them with others; (10) It is never too late to reach out and do the right thing; pride, or alienation, or bias, or status should not stand in the way of doing the right thing; (11) Working in the medical field, particularly in pre-natal and geriatrics patients, there are thousands of miracles every day, and in being thankful for those miracles that we take for granted; (12) Life is too short to be feeling sorry for myself, or blaming others, or engaging in analysis paralysis, or endless discussions; (13) the need to be selective and in cultivating, nurturing, and protecting the best relationships and networks; (14) Learning from my mistakes; (15) Protecting my brand; (16) Being rejected or abandoned is part of life, the world does not end there, do not take it personally, get over it, keep searching, be patient and move on; and, (17) Life consists of several cycles of ups and downs.

- One of the many principles to keep in mind is the second law of thermodynamics. Nature goes from order to disorder.
- I can now better appreciate the blank stares from Mr. Abanilla, Mr. Santiago, Mrs. Abaya, Mrs. Gamalinda, Mr. Capayas – all of whom were about 60 years or older when we were 14-16 years old in 1969. How I wish to be able to talk to them and compare notes after earning several black eyes, bloody noses and arrows behind our back in behaving in juvenile and arrogant ways 44 years ago.
- To all my mentors, supporters:

You Raise Me Up – Josh Groban

http://www.youtube.com/watch?v=6VqRlO3wa1A

When I am down and, oh my soul, so weary;
When troubles come and my heart burdened be;
Then, I am still and wait here in the silence,
Until you come and sit awhile with me.

You raise me up, so I can stand on mountains;
You raise me up, to walk on stormy seas;
I am strong, when I am on your shoulders;
You raise me up... To more than I can be.

You raise me up, so I can stand on mountains;
You raise me up, to walk on stormy seas;
I am strong, when I am on your shoulders;
You raise me up... To more than I can be.

(continued...)

- For added perspective, let me share the partial lyrics of the 3 songs that most remind me of our batch and the years we were together:

First Of May Lyrics – Sarah Brightman

  http://www.youtube.com/watch?v=kjEwqpyzU1k

When I was small, and Christmas trees were tall,
We used to love while others used to play.
Don't ask me why, but time has passed us by,
Someone else moved in from far away.

Now we are tall, and Christmas trees are small,
And you don't ask the time of day.
But you and I, our love will never die,
But guess well cry come first of may.

(continued...)

MacArthur Park – Richard Harris

  http://www.youtube.com/watch?v=amzJDSsC2IA

Someone left the cake out in the rain
I don't think that I can take it
'Cause it took so long to bake it
And I'll never have that recipe again
Oh, no!

(continued...)

Greenfields – Brothers Four

  http://www.youtube.com/watch?v=46o1joHp7t0

Once they were part of an everlasting love
We were the lovers who strolled through green fields
Green fields are gone now, parched by the sun

Gone from the valleys where rivers used to run
Gone with the cold wind that swept into my heart
Gone with the lovers who let their dreams depart
Where are the green fields that we used to roam

(continued...)

- If the objective of this Reunion is primarily reconnect and revisit what we shared during those years past, share stories and laughter - I believe, we succeeded. But if the objective is to prepare and pass on to the next generation the blessings and fortunes that we had, I am not sure that as a community, we have anything close to what other communities have been doing successfully for hundreds or thousands of years. I am hoping that our narratives will be a step in that direction.

In the autumn of our lives, how many of us associate ourselves with Schmidt in the "About Schmidt" movie?
- Speaking of looking back, I wish I know 1% of 1% of what I know today way back in high school. I would have taken a different path and done things differently. However, these would not necessarily make me a better and stronger person. In my case at least, the level of unpredictability, adversities and challenges made me a stronger and a sensitive person.
- Whenever I feel sad and desperately in need of inspiration, whenever I needed a place of refuge and solace, I fondly look back and travel 44 years ago, selectively fast forward to the present, and fast backward, listen to the music and lyrics, watch the movies of those times – and reminisce those days, the specifics of which I shared with you through this narrative today. This is the impact of the UECHS batch of 69 to who I am today... Thank you for your time.

    - The Mentor from California

The Most Memorable Music of Our Times

The musical pieces below are part of the narratives. These are the music and lyrics that resonate the most among the narrators, and are universal and timeless across generations.

A HOUSE IS NOT A HOME – SHIRLEY BASSEY

http://www.youtube.com/watch?v=azPuqNiNNh0

ALL ALONE AM I – BRENDA LEE

http://www.youtube.com/watch?v=wnApJcGBDFY

AND I LOVE YOU SO – SHIRLEY BASSEY

http://www.youtube.com/watch?v=rc5m8b4fWQM

ALL ALONE AM I – BRENDA LEE

http://www.youtube.com/watch?v=JJHvYU_y6xQ

AMAZING GRACE – SOWETO GOSPEL CHOIR; HAYLE WESTENRA

http://www.youtube.com/watch?v=ZoJz2SANTyo
http://www.youtube.com/watch?v=5mnTKN8LuiY

ANNIE'S SONG – JOHN DENVER

http://www.youtube.com/watch?v=HkGS263lGsQ

AVE MARIA – BARBARA BOONEY, HELEN FISCHER

http://www.youtube.com/watch?v=aQVz6vuNq7s
http://www.youtube.com/watch?v=OxjJFB-j5RU

BOTH SIDES NOW – JUDI COLLINS

http://www.youtube.com/watch?v=z8jGFu7ys64

BRIDGE OVER TROUBLED WATER – SIMON AND GARFUNKLE

http://www.youtube.com/watch?v=UVDg8fVC4EQ

BRING HIM HOME, LES MISERABLES – ALPHI BOE & MORMON TABERNACLE

http://www.youtube.com/watch?v=tI4jb-Aca9M

CLIMB EVERY MOUNTAIN – JULIE ANDREWS

http://www.youtube.com/watch?v=EoCPuhhE6dw

CLOSE TO YOU - CARPENTERS

http://www.youtube.com/watch?v=oaOyoVS-IAI

CRAZY – PATSY CLINE

http://www.youtube.com/watch?v=6QEDb3xzdec

DANNY BOY – ANY WILLIAMS

http://www.youtube.com/watch?v=ujr8dQJgQUU

DEVOTED TO YOU – CARLY SIMON & JAMES TAYLOR

http://www.youtube.com/watch?v=K_IK41kC15g

DID'NT WE – RICHARD HARRIS, JOHNNY MATHIS

http://www.youtube.com/watch?v=3BQSFlfK2rg
http://www.youtube.com/watch?v=FMj-F9-ttlc

DO YOU LOVE ME? – FIDDLER ON THE ROOF

http://www.youtube.com/watch?v=h_y9F5St4j0

END OF THE WORLD – SKEETER DAVIS

http://www.youtube.com/watch?v=NZ5WeXtOacU

ERES TU - MOCEDADES

http://www.youtube.com/watch?v=1s3BIX0duKs

FATHER AND SON – CAT STEVENS

http://www.youtube.com/watch?v=Q29YR5-t3gg

FIRST OF MAY – SARAH BRIGHTMAN

http://www.youtube.com/watch?v=kjEwgpyzU1k

FIVE HUNDRED (500) MILES – BROTHERS FOUR

http://www.youtube.com/watch?v=B_K6z3HiRAs
http://www.youtube.com/watch?v=VLeyCX3Em-c

GOING HOME - DVORAK

http://www.youtube.com/watch?v=o2aLSat3h0w
http://www.youtube.com/watch?v=EcvKdMtYei0
http://www.youtube.com/watch?v=iJFhTb1gi6Y
http://www.youtube.com/watch?v=I9ChiBPJgmg
http://www.youtube.com/watch?v=M9smSP1dq-A
http://www.youtube.com/watch?v=W19CU3zwxkM

HELLO – LIONEL RICHIE

http://www.youtube.com/watch?v=PDZcqBgCS74

HOMEWARD BOUND – SIMON AND GARFUNKLE

http://www.youtube.com/watch?v=U6K8wfyzAJQ
http://www.youtube.com/watch?v=4EgRT6bVIZo

HONEY – BOBBY GOLDSBORO

http://www.youtube.com/watch?v=59BZxgohr9g

HOW AM I SUPPOSED TO LIVE WITHOUT YOU – HELEN FISCHER AND MICHAEL BOLTON

http://www.youtube.com/watch?v=qFhFujPcaGo

I BELIEVE – TOM JONES

http://www.youtube.com/watch?v=Sv3A_ABxZLQ

I DID IT MY WAY – FRANK SINATRA

http://www.youtube.com/watch?v=egY8rUpxqcE

I DREAMED A DREAM – ANNA HATHAWAY & HAYLE WESTENRA

http://www.youtube.com/watch?v=SyQ-0JOF1Qk
http://www.youtube.com/watch?v=ZSwx2MdUKzw
http://www.youtube.com/watch?v=7JP3AVGW9hM

I HAVE A DREAM – ABBA

http://www.youtube.com/watch?v=r82fyOb8F5w

IF I EVER I WOULD LEAVE YOU – ROBERT GOULET

http://www.youtube.com/watch?v=xL52hEArSfM

I'LL NEVER FIND ANOTHER YOU – THE SEEKERS

http://www.youtube.com/watch?v=4Ga9Bs4fzSY

I STARTED A JOKE – BEE GEES

http://www.youtube.com/watch?v=8Ye1bJr0q-0

IT MUST BE HIM – VIKKI CARR

http://www.youtube.com/watch?v=kWvpJ5AY3mE

ITSY BITSY SPIDER – CARLY SIMON

http://www.youtube.com/watch?v=-J_9kYdRFCM

I WHO HAVE NOTHING – TOM JONES & SHIRLEY BASSEY

http://www.youtube.com/watch?v=9rgLd6A0DWM
http://www.youtube.com/watch?v=Wc9Q_ncWQfw

IMAGINE – JOHN LENNON

http://www.youtube.com/watch?v=XLgYAHHkPFs

I WILL WAIT FOR YOU - LAINIE KAZAN

http://www.youtube.com/watch?v=ozkGBZpkYsE

KILLING ME SOFTLY WITH HIS SONG – ROBERTA FLACK

http://www.youtube.com/watch?v=LQ2t5e7stVM

LEAVING ON A JET PLANE – PETER, PAUL & MARY

    http://www.youtube.com/watch?v=HIshbtQ6LgA

LOVE STORY – ANY WILLIAMS

    http://www.youtube.com/watch?v=5A1KZKksGKE

MACARTHUR PARK – RICHARD HARRIS

    http://www.youtube.com/watch?v=amzJDSsC2IA

MAKE IT UP TO YOU – THE BREAD

    http://www.youtube.com/watch?v=K4R93xnKink

MEMORIES – BARBARA STREISAND

    http://www.youtube.com/watch?v=n-KPGh3wysw

MEMORIES – CATS

    http://www.youtube.com/watch?v=4-L6rEm0rnY

MORNING HAS BROKEN – CAT STEVENS

    http://www.youtube.com/watch?v=U5sSEkZ86ts

NO MAN IS AN ISLAND – THE LETTERMEN

    http://www.youtube.com/watch?v=hWlMfmsIW8U

OVER THE RAINBOW – ISRAEL "IZ" KAMAKAWIWO'OLE

    http://www.youtube.com/watch?v=w_DKWlrA24k

PILIPINAS KONG MAHAL; BAYAN KO

    http://ofcintl.org/

ONCE THERE WERE GREENFIELDS – BROTHERS 4

    http://www.youtube.com/watch?v=46o1joHp7t0

OSCAR HAMMERSTEIN MEDLEY

http://www.youtube.com/watch?v=xCdyRq_eZkY

SAD MOVIES (Make Me Cry) – SUE THOMPSON

http://www.youtube.com/watch?v=XFMfx1Y-aj0

SHENANDOAH – BROTHERS FOUR

http://www.youtube.com/watch?v=zFIK2EPzeJo

SOMEWHERE MY LOVE - LARA'S THEME IN DR. ZHIVAGO, RAY CONNIFF

http://www.youtube.com/watch?v=6iV_MEy91tQ

SOUND OF SILENCE – SIMON AND GARFUNKLE

http://www.youtube.com/watch?v=0jqn9SKYAgY

SUMMER SONG – CHAD & JEREMY

http://www.youtube.com/watch?v=VvD0_aeAf2E

SUNRISE, SUNSET – FIDDLER ON THE ROOF, PERRY COMO, ROBERT GOULET

http://www.youtube.com/watch?v=nLLEBAQLZ3Q
http://www.youtube.com/watch?v=nsQroDvqQAE
http://www.youtube.com/watch?v=vWtKKPCKCIA
http://www.youtube.com/watch?v=36R93Vk0nAY

TAKE ME HOME – JOHN DENVER

http://www.youtube.com/watch?v=6WmgmTFkG9Q

TENNESSEE WALTZ - Patti Page

http://www.youtube.com/watch?v=_Ek3eCbfqp0

THE FIRST TIME I SAW YOUR FACE – ROBERTA FLACK

http://www.youtube.com/watch?v=hOFrGbuUqnQ

THE GREEN GRASS OF HOME – JOAN BAEZ

http://www.youtube.com/watch?v=aQhKqlOccHE

THE GREEN LEAVES OF SUMMER – PATTI PAGE; BROTHERS FOUR

http://www.youtube.com/watch?v=-GkL_GiVjWk
http://www.youtube.com/watch?v=_xXGjSH3lmc

THE IMPOSSIBLE DREAM – LUTHER VANDROSS

http://www.youtube.com/watch?v=AijRBQf-ato

THE MARCH – CHOPIN

http://www.youtube.com/watch?v=kyFyAqLtHq8

THE POWER OF LOVE - HELENE FISCHER

http://www.youtube.com/watch?v=0AwYVMgYw60

THE PRAYER – HELEN FISCHER, MICHAEL BOLTON, ANDREA BOCELLI

http://www.youtube.com/watch?v=D8C7hu-HF2E
http://www.youtube.com/watch?v=85aREalo2PE

THE ROSE – BETTER MIDLER

http://www.youtube.com/watch?v=Zf5UfOuvQHQ

THIS IS MY LIFE – SHIRLEY BASSEY

http://www.youtube.com/watch?v=XwcOqUlLjLk

THIS IS MY SONG – PETULA CLARK

http://www.youtube.com/watch?v=V8XmLuTmKIM

THIS LAND IS YOUR LAND – BROTHERS FOUR

http://www.youtube.com/watch?v=kLXz1FJMKRw

THOSE WERE THE DAYS – MARY HOPKIN

http://www.youtube.com/watch?v=gVdOQvx379Y

TIME TO SAY GOOD BYE - HELENE FISCHER, SARAH BRIGHTMAN, ANDREA BOCELLI

http://www.youtube.com/watch?v=khznWuH3VTs
http://www.youtube.com/watch?v=X0yjip9IKA4

TO SIR WITH LOVE – LULU

http://www.youtube.com/watch?v=sczEBtOnD3k

TURN AROUND – BROTHERS FOUR

http://www.youtube.com/watch?v=Kb6mlPFzkx0

UNCHAINED MELODY – RIGHTEOUS BROTHERS

http://www.youtube.com/watch?v=zrK5u5W8afc

WE SHALL OVERCOME

http://www.youtube.com/watch?v=RkNsEH1GD7Q

WHEN I FALL IN LOVE – LETTERMEN & NAT KING COLE

http://www.youtube.com/watch?v=Dq4PDKDsW-s
http://www.youtube.com/watch?v=GfAb0gNPy6s

WHERE HAVE ALL THE FLOWERS GONE – BROTHERS FOUR, PETER, PAUL & MARY

http://www.youtube.com/watch?v=HyG28T8WcNM
http://www.youtube.com/watch?v=1QZq-wKaBWc

WE'VE ONLY JUST BEGAN - CARPENTERS

http://www.youtube.com/watch?v=__VQX2Xn7tI

WILL YOU STILL LOVE ME TOMORROW

http://www.youtube.com/watch?v=pB8Mu_rnbLc

WIND BENEATH MY WINGS – BETTE MIDLER

http://www.youtube.com/watch?v=5RMrltCDCwI
http://www.youtube.com/watch?v=VWqB-6ANG4c

WOMAN – PETER & GORDON

http://www.youtube.com/watch?v=mEr76NhLaUY

WONDERFUL WORLD – LOUIS ARMSTRONG

http://www.youtube.com/watch?v=E2VCwBzGdPM

WORDS – BEE GEES

http://www.youtube.com/watch?v=M92QzPjgbag

YESTERDAY WHEN I WAS YOUNG – SHIRLEY BASSEY & CHARLES AZNAVOUR

http://www.youtube.com/watch?v=kz_2EonNxpQ

YOU DON'T HAVE TO SAY YOU LOVE ME – DUSTY SPRINGFIELD

http://www.youtube.com/watch?v=l9NY3P1QwWw

YOU RAISE ME UP – JOSH GROBAN

http://www.youtube.com/watch?v=6VqRlO3wa1A

YOU'RE SO VAIN – CARLY SIMON

http://www.youtube.com/watch?v=b6UAYGxiRwU

YOU'LL NEVER WALK ALONE – MORMON TABERNACLE, REGINE VELASQUEZ, TOM JONES

http://www.youtube.com/watch?v=ky8_CZ4Y5Sg
http://www.youtube.com/watch?v=ec8oKBzF1Bo
http://www.youtube.com/watch?v=dSeZdqSsyRI

YOU'VE GOT A FRIEND – CAROL KING, JAMES TAYLOR

http://www.youtube.com/watch?v=qde5NMy7WTU
http://www.youtube.com/watch?v=3WJ1cf3nrLE
http://www.youtube.com/watch?v=rJPgxEi2BM8

www.ingramcontent.com/pod-product-compliance
Lightning Source LLC
Chambersburg PA
CBHW032027090426
42741CB00006B/762